EDINBURGH'S CHILD

EDINBURGH'S CHILD

Some memories of ninety years

ELEANOR SILLAR

Illustrations by
OLIVER HOLT

OLIVER AND BOYD
EDINBURGH AND LONDON

OLIVER AND BOYD LTD.

Tweeddale Court
Edinburgh

39a Welbeck Street
London, W. 1

| First Published | .. | .. | .. | 1961 |
| Reprinted | .. | .. | .. | 1961 |

Printed in Great Britain
by T. and A. CONSTABLE LTD., Hopetoun Street,
Printers to the University of Edinburgh

TO MY FAMILY

FOREWORD

I wrote the essays which have been collected together in this book mainly for my own pleasure, perhaps to remind myself of the happinesses of my early days in Edinburgh, while my memory of them was still clear. Then, later, as they grew, I began to think that they might be of interest to my children and my friends. It was my son who felt that they would have an interest beyond the family circle and should be published.

The Edinburgh which these memoirs describe is no more, but the memory remains. It is in the recording of such memories that the great traditions by which we live can be preserved.

I am most grateful to my friend Oliver Holt for his charming drawings, which help so much to make these memory pictures vivid.

E.F.S.

CONTENTS

EDINBURGH'S CHILD

Many years ago, in Edinburgh, there might have been seen walking, daily and unhurriedly, through her wide streets and stately squares, a little group of three. Myself, my little brother Louis, and Ann, our Nurse.

In the light of other, far elder days, I look back and smile to see the little girl who was me, passing along, rapt in childish dreams, all unaware of the beauty that encompassed her.

The beauty that was Edinburgh; austere, but vivid, often startling. Grey fortress set aloft on the grey precipice, the flash of sunlit greenery in the gardens below; breath-taking vistas of sea and hills; high skies, and sea winds blowing. Edinburgh, Scotland's history in her every grey stone, with her grave and kindly people, and her heritage of lore and learning, looking out for ever northwards across the Firth of Forth, and southwards to the Pentland Hills, towards

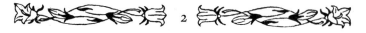

which her suburbs, like long fingers, stretch out to touch the heather.

Edinburgh, my background.

The eyes and mind of a little child are apt to take in the smaller, more intimate things around them, and pay little heed to the greater. But all the time the greater things are there, and rain influence; for me, shaping for good and all my loves and tastes, my understanding, my whole life.

A little later, and there came a day when my eyes were opened; when, standing at some high corner of George Street, I looked down the long slope leading by gardens and pleasant dwellings to the shore, where Newhaven sends out the brown-sailed fishing-boats, and across the blue Firth I saw, and wondered at the dreaming hills of Fife. Then was born in me a consciousness of space and mystery. Then did I begin to understand the strange and haunting sense of "over the hills and far away".

But that day was not yet.

March winds blowing, blowing, brilliant gleams of sunshine. Ann, in her fawn-coloured shawl with a fringe, is a nice leisurely person as she walks with a child on either side, their hands in hers. We were not dragged along, weary and unwilling.

I thought Louis adorable in his dark blue coat and scarlet stockings, with the Glengarry bonnet on his long yellow curls. But I hated my own coat of black Persian lamb cloth, which I called my "curly jacket".

In the summer days we played in the Queen Street Gardens, to us an immense country, where the shrubberies of rhododendrons had the half-fearful charm of unexplored

forests, and the lawns seemed endless stretches of grass and daisies.

But in winter, and now, when the March winds blew, we turned the corner out of York Place, our home street, and so up into St. Andrew Square. We went into Law's Coffee Shop, which was very dignified, and had a pillared portico and big doors. Inside the shop we were plunged into a delicious atmosphere of freshly-ground coffee. But, for Louis and me, the whole purpose of the shop was not the coffee, but the cat. Huge, grey, splendid, he was the pet of every customer. But I sometimes wonder if he was really as enormous as my memory paints him! He would come bounding out of the hidden depths of the back premises, nearly knocking us down with friendliness, purring loudly as we daringly stroked his beautiful fur. It was like fondling a tiger.

Outside Law's, close to the edge of the pavement, sat the Blind Man on his stool, reading the Bible aloud, his not very clean fingers moving across the page. Nobody ever saw him turn the page. He was a cantankerous old creature, and had never a "thank you" for the penny I would drop into the plate beside him. But the charitable act gave me a pleasant sense of patronage.

For Louis and me the St. Andrew Square Gardens, spacious, green-lawned, their privacy ensured by elegant iron railings, were bare of interest, for no children ever played in them. In the centre the fluted columns of the Melville Monument seemed in our eyes to rise to endless heights.

I have one vivid memory of that column, of a night when I stood holding on to my father's hand and saw it towering

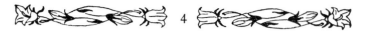

into the night sky like a pillar of fire, every carven groove, from top to bottom, ablaze with coloured lights. There was excitement in the air, there were crowds, and cheers and rockets flaring to heaven and bursting into stars of green and red. What was it all about? My childish ears caught words like "marriage" and "princess" in the grown-up people's talk. The Duke of Edinburgh married the Russian Princess Alexandrovna in 1874. Could that have been the reason for all this excitement, which has given me such a memory of magnificence? I would be just five years old.

Down into Princes Street, in those days the leisurely promenade of leisurely people, doing their leisurely shopping. Spring sunshine, spring dresses, spring green along the mile of gardens facing the mile of shops, charming shops, but for Louis and me just shops, all in the day's walk. Now the toyshop in Hanover Street was the shop of "Dreams-Come-True", where golden minutes sped by as we admired and longed and at long last chose, some one among the penny treasures spread out for our delight. There were times when, with the occasional sixpence, wealth unspeakable, in my hand, I played the spendthrift, laying it out in one fell swoop on the doll of my desire, waxen, pink, blonde, blue-eyed. I remember a succession of these.

The toy-shop was *down* some wide stone steps, and next door, *up* some wide stone steps, was Vallance's the sweetie-shop—Louis and I had each a halfpenny to spend on toffee-drops. Ann considered toffee-drops to be wholesome. Our mouths watering, we would watch the lady behind the counter twist up, with incredible speed and dexterity, two paper pokes, then pop in the toffee-drops and hand them

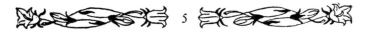

over to us. She smiled, Ann smiled, we smiled, and sucked on our succulent way in great content.

But far and beyond all ordinary shops, wonderful but transient, was Kennington and Jenner's Christmas Bazaar. As we walked along, in this time of daffodils and March winds, that Bazaar seemed like a vision of glory for ever vanished.

A vision—of Princes Street on a frosty afternoon, sky reddening to the early winter sunset, one's breath like smoke. "Papa" in holiday humour swinging his stick, joking as we danced along at his side. Here we are! Up the shallow stone steps, through the glass doors and the jostling throng of grown-up shoppers. We pitied them, Louis and I. They seemed so unaware of the world of glories beneath their very feet. We knew better.

Down and down the unfamiliar stairs, leaving behind us the light of day and the frosty air, plunging into what was surely the magic cavern of all the fairy-tales, a region where innumerable gas jets lit up a Paradise, sparkling on the strings of many-coloured glass balls which crossed and re-crossed the low ceiling, gleaming on rows of golden-haired dolls, glittering on toys and tinsel.

A multitude of children push, gazing and wondering, this way and that, struggling to get near the popular "Penny Stall". One penny each! Penny whips and whistles! Penny dolls and donkeys! Penny popguns and pistols!

Louis loves a popgun. But at another stall, where all the joys of childhood seem piled one above another high above my head, I stop.

"This lovely rabbit?" says the nice woman holding it out tempting and ingratiating. "Half a crown!"

I gasp, but Papa jovially hands over the money.

With my treasure pressed close against my "curly jacket" and under my chin, I move, and breathe, and see the world through an ecstasy of soft whiteness.

"Will Christmas Bazaar come again?" we ask, seeing the daffodils, and holding on to our hats in the wind.

"Aye will it," says Ann, "next Christmas. So that." Ann often ends her sentences that way. Like "Selah" in the Psalms.

Down into Princes Street, where the horse-drawn carriages and tramway cars seemed to us a crowded traffic. Just across from the corner of St. Andrew Street was the flat roof of the Waverley Market, with roof windows sticking up here and there, and ingenious little borders where geraniums were planted in summer. We crossed over just where it seemed good to us. No policeman held up his hand to stop us.

But accidents did sometimes happen. Once, on our usual walk, we saw one. A tramway car just starting—a little ragged girl darting out to cross in front of it—a shrill screaming—the driver shouting and reining in two plunging horses—a crowd—Ann, exclaiming in horror and pity and holding tightly on to Louis and me on the pavement—and then—a policeman pushing his way through the crowd, holding a little bundle in his arms—a glimpse of a white face, and the sound of moaning. The policeman with his pitiful burden gets into a cab and drives away.

"Where to?" we ask, terror-stricken.

"To the Infirmary," says Ann sadly. "Puir bairn!"

Beside the Waverley Market were the Waverley Steps, where we gazed down long flights of stone stairs, which

disappeared into mysterious fascinating depths, whence came
the sounds of explosive puffings and whistlings, and we
caught tantalising glimpses of funnels and smoke. Round
the corner on to what we knew as "the Bridges". We could
not see over the parapet, but we could hear the trains
rumbling along below us. On up the narrow street to
Harrison the tailor's shop, where Louis and I were to be
measured for new ulsters. Mr. Hodges set us on two high
chairs and bowed over the counter to Ann, spreading out
rolls of cloth.

Mr. George Harrison came out of his little office at the
back of the shop, like a mouse out of its hole. He rubbed his
hands and joked with us. We knew his father was the
Lord Provost, which we thought must be grander than
a king. But we could not guess that our friend in the shop,
with the red whiskers and a frock-coat, would himself
be Lord Provost one day and wear a scarlet gown and
ermine.

It was steep going up to the top where the High Street,
crossed the tram-lines. We watched a pair of tram-horses,
poor panting beasts, straining up the hill with a dead weight
of car and passengers behind them, and helped by what we
knew as a trace-horse hitched on to the centre pole, and
ridden by a jovial raggamuffin of a boy, who egged on the
team, with yells and whip-crackings. At the top he un-
hitched his tackle, and went clattering and jingling down the
hill again ready for the next load. I regarded that boy with
deep envy. His seemed to me to be the perfect life.

We came to the High Street, that long grey mile of tall
grey houses, dark with age and secrets, stretching from the
Castle down to Holyrood Palace.

B

The tall grey houses looked down on me as they had looked down on all those others who had passed beneath them through the long years.

"Once upon a time," they whispered. But for me "once upon a time" led to Fairyland, not to History. I had no vision of gay gallants in velvet and lace, roystering down the Canongate. I heard no clash of swords in the dark entries of the "Closes". I saw no Bonny Prince Charlie on his charger among the shouting crowds, riding, with eyes turned upward to the high windows of these same grey houses, where white hands waved in greeting—I only saw, with absorbed interest, the bare-footed children playing "peevers" on the pavement.

The ghosts of long-ago Edinburgh walked beside me, and I paid no heed. The laughter, the tragedy, the bravery of past days were round about me, were part of me, though a knew it not. I could not escape.

"We'll look in at McLaren's," said Ann, and so we turned right, uphill towards the Lawnmarket and the Castle.

McLaren's was a very grand draper's shop, in spite of its locality. Out of the fortune made there, emerged, in the fullness of time, a very learned judge. But for me it was just Mr. Brown's shop. Mr. Brown was Ann's brother-in-law. So we "looked in" to see Mr. Brown. I remember well the long polished mahogany counters and the tiers upon tiers of mahogany drawers with brass handles.

We saw Mr. Brown, and others like him, being very busy and civil behind the counters trying to please the lady customers, who were in no hurry to be pleased.

Mr. Brown saw us, and left his customers to come and speak to us. As far as I knew he owned the whole shop

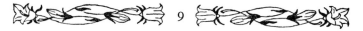

and everything in it. So I felt very grand and important and hoped all the lady customers observed and envied.

Across the street the great doors of St. Giles' Cathedral face us, stern, uncompromising—but, in contradiction, far above our heads, the gentle delicate chimes tell out the hours to the skies.

Round the echoing colonnade of the Parliament House ran Louis and I, rejoicing, though a policeman frowned. In a wide corridor we peeped through the glass doors of the great hall, where the advocates in their wigs and gowns paced up and down, up and down, unceasingly.

Children have their own landmarks in their ordinary walks abroad. Ferguson's, the Edinburgh Rock Shop, was one of ours. Here it is we turn to go downhill homewards. So we do. But in turning, I cast longing eyes up the steep Lawnmarket. The Castle is up there. I had been there with Papa. I had seen the soldiers drilling on the Esplanade, and wondered how the sentries could stand so stiff and still. And somewhere up there I remember a great wide stone place with a parapet, where the guns are, with Mons Meg, the huge old Monster Gun, on guard behind them. I remember how I climbed on Mons Meg, and for a blissful minute rode triumphant. Now, as I hold Ann's hand, I dream again of that high Battery, so remote, so quiet, seeming, for all the guns being there, a platform of peace. Up there (I dream) the sky leans down to me and I hear Papa say.

"Look! You can see the Highland hills!"

Too far, too far. Not in my world. Not yet, for me the lure of wide horizons.

I peer over the parapet, down cliff and precipice to the

tops of trees, and under them green lawns, and over above them a street.

"Princes Street", says Papa.

I gaze and think, *that* Princes Street? Can that be *my* Princes Street? Where I walk with Ann nearly every day? That little street?

East End, West End, I can see both ends at once! When I am down there, I am just a very little girl, and East End, West End are mere vanishing points in dim distances. And oh! the weary way between them!

And down there, that very little girl sees the houses, with the shop-windows beside the pavement, towering high above her head, with their far off top windows like blind eyes staring into space.

But up here! oh, up here! she laughs at these tall houses, so aloof, so proud. She thinks, up here the secrets of their roofs are all mine! Their chimneys are just like rows of smoking teeth!

Down there, how big the carriages are! How huge the horses! How noisy the tramway cars! How the air is full of clip-cloppings, bangings and bells!

But up here! Why, they are just so many gently jingling toys! Up here, the little girl that is me looks down and sees all the people like puppets, passing and repassing, going in and out of shops, stopping to talk to friends, and she laughs again. She says to herself, "These funny little people down there don't know I am watching them! I see them, but they don't see me!" That thought gives the little girl a strange feeling of power.

So, still dreaming my dreams, I am led by Ann down the curving way of the Mound, homewards.

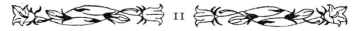

II

Suddenly, from away along Princes Street, comes the sound of drums beating. The wind blowing our curls, blows to our ears the skirling of the pipes. The Highlanders! We see them now! There they come, marching down the middle of the street, hemmed in by vociferous satellites, men and boys. Splendid noise, coming nearer! How one's heart beats with the beating of the drums! Round the corner, magnificently wheeling, they take the hill by storm. Ann holds up Louis. I stand on tiptoe. Ecstatic moment! They are before us, passing us, tartans waving, pibroch sounding, white gaiters flashing to the quick step. A joyful pageant for childish eyes! Like a many-coloured serpent they wind steeply up to the Castle. Our eyes follow them. Going, going, gone! The music of the pipes takes on a "dying fall", and the drums are no longer a sound but a throb.

"We maun awa' hame now," says Ann.

March winds blowing, blowing. Into my mind come thoughts of nursery play, and a clean pinafore, and dessert in the dining-room with Papa and my big brothers.

The daffodils on the banks toss as if they would toss their heads off. Young buds on the trees are shaken. Westwards, where I know the Corstorphine Hill is, delicate clouds are reddening. Midway in the East Princes Street Gardens, the Scott Monument, like a well-sharpened pencil, is pointing, as it seems to me, not *at* but *into* the late afternoon sky. At the corner of Hanover Street sits the old piper, in his plaid and bonnet, his silver hair and beard blown and tangled. His head is bowed over his beloved pipes, dinned into silence by those passing bands.

Home. Ann opens the front door with her key, and we rush in with shouts. The day's walk is ended.

"So that!" sighs Ann, and shuts the door.

Comes bed-time; night closing round. Outside the nursery windows darkness, and the stars.

Edinburgh's child sleeps. But Edinburgh, cradling her child, sleeps not.

Edinburgh, beautiful for situation, throned among the hills, having the sea for footstool, sleeps never.

Out in the Forth, Inchkeith and the May, her outposts, flash their warnings to the ships. High up in the Castle, far above her child's head, the watch is set.

ROUND AND ABOUT THE HOUSE

A little girl of three, both her hands stretched up and held by a grown-up person on either side, gazed along what seemed an endless vista of broad grey street. Such is an early, vague memory of myself and of what I came to know as "York Place". As the years passed, that memory became the background of many memories, more definite, more solid, indelible, perhaps eternal.

61 York Place, Edinburgh, the home of my youth, with the shallow, stone steps leading up to the wide, dignified door. A wide front door has ever to me a welcoming air, a promise of hospitality, kindly and generous. And indeed up those steps came, through the years, many a gay guest, passing on through the wide door flung open to receive them, into the warm and gracious hall, and upstairs to the bright lights, the voices and laughter, of the drawing-room.

Immediately opposite to the house, across what to my childish eyes was an immense width, paved with grey stone "setts", stood St. Paul's church—our church, to which, even when very young, we were taken every Sunday by my father, the Sheriff. St. Paul's was on the sunny side of the street, facing the south. "61" faced the cold north, and if St. Paul's had not been there we could have seen, from our drawing-room windows, down the long slope of trees and houses away to the grey Forth and across to the Fife hills. On many a cold autumn night have I stood at one of those windows and watched the flashing and flickering of the Northern Lights above St. Paul's.

The street ran east and west, the north side on a lower level than the south, and its tall grey houses had, I think, a greater air of aristocratic aloofness than those on our side, where some had been made into flats, and had common stairs. One of these common stairs was next door to "61", leading up to a flat which by rights should have been the top part of our house. The people living in that flat used to have dances, and as our nursery was just below the room they danced in, often and often have I lain awake through the long evening listening to the strumming of a piano overhead, and the thumping of feet, which so shook the ceiling that I lay in constant dread lest it should come crashing down on me and Louis. But these York Place houses were built with walls so solid, with floors so strong and yet so elastic, that not even a crack showed in the plaster.

The two tall windows of the big nursery looked south, over the backgreen to a lane, ever to me mysterious, for the high wall hid it, and the door in the wall was never open that I can remember. But there were sounds that came from the lane: the rattle of the coal carts on dark winter mornings, and the coalman's harsh cry, in untuneful seconds, "Ca-ool! Ca-ool!"

At the far side of the lane, just beyond our wall, could be seen the side-wall and windows of the Roman Catholic pro-cathedral, and the door and windows of the Priests' House. Beyond these, and dominating them, rose the high roof of the Theatre Royal. We were close enough to hear sometimes the shouts and clapping of hands; and I remember the dreadful noise at, I think, the destruction of Nineveh, in the play of "Sardanapalus". Charlie had been taken to see it, probably on its first night, and then gave us so graphic a description of its excitement and terror, that for the rest of the week of its performance in the theatre, when the sound of the yells and crashes in the final scene shook the quiet of the darkened nursery, I held my breath in fear. Different indeed was the Sunday sound of the organ and choir in the pro-Cathedral, especially on the Sunday of the week when the Carl Rosa Opera Company were performing in the theatre, for members of it used on that day to sing in the choir. In this way came perhaps some of my earliest musical thrills, when Handel's "Hallelujah Chorus" rang out in, to me, an unaccustomed glory of sound, across the lane and the backgreen, and in at the nursery windows, tremendous above the low thunder of the organ.

About the roof of the Theatre Royal there comes to me a clear and startling memory. One Saturday morning, when I was about five years old, in coming in from our morning walk with Ann, the nursery door was opened, and we stood suddenly aghast, staring at the familiar room lit up by a strange and terrifying crimson glow. Louis and I rushed to the window, crying out at the sight of the leaping flames and columns of thick smoke rising from the theatre roof. I remember the excited interest of everyone, and the exclamations of Ann and the other maids as the roof fell in with a crash: my father's uneasiness as the window-panes grew hot: the coming in of a fireman to see that all was safe: and the restless night that followed that day of alarms, with the noise of engines and the crackle of fire lasting well into the night: the shouts in the street, and then the dawn breaking with the acrid smell of burnt and smouldering ruins.

There was an aspect of this theatre fire that filled the minds of those about me, and which therefore impressed itself deeply on my mind. Charlie and I had been in the theatre the very night before the fire, watching the Pantomime from the stage box, and had been taken at the end behind the scenes by Mr. and Mrs. Wyndham, and had gazed, thrilled and wondering, up into the dark spaces of ropes and pulleys and huge canvas. And the next day all these were smoking ruins. According to everyone, Charlie and I had a marvellous escape. Indeed Aunt Louisa, who thought theatres were wicked places, was convinced that it was only by a special mercy of Providence that we had not been burnt alive with the theatre.

Our backgreen was a spacious one. You reached it by running down the kitchen stairs, then out at the back door of the long passage, across the area and up a flight of stone steps. A broad border ran along the breadth next the house, where in summer we planted red daisies and all kinds of pansies, bought in the Saturday market. At the far end of the green were two trees, a lilac and a laburnum. Although the leaves and branches were grimy with town soot, I swear that I have never seen anything brighter than the golden glory of the tassels of that laburnum tree, nor smelt anything sweeter than the bunches we picked off that lilac.

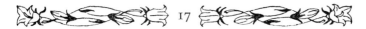

Ann did not approve of our playing in the backgreen. I
suppose the soot came off on our hands and pinafores. But
there were summer evenings when my father would sally
forth to smoke his after-dinner pipe, a long churchwarden,
sitting in a chair under the trees; and with his indulgent eye
upon us, we would for a short but gleeful half-hour defy all
nursery rules. On these rare occasions the mere back view of
the house seemed to have something interesting and exciting
about it. It had an air at once homelier and more intimate
than the formal front so familiar to us—just as if the house
had put off its robes of ceremony and donned its more work-
a-day garments. Seen from the backgreen, even our nursery
windows looked pleasantly strange. There indeed was the
cage of turtle doves on the top of the toy-cupboard, but the
back view of the cage looked somehow odd and different,
and the turtle doves themselves turned their tail-feathers
window-wards, and did their cooings and bowings always
towards the room.

The kitchen looked out on the back area, which was wide
and light. White flag-stones, table and long dresser like
snow, shining pans and lids polished to dazzle the eye and
reflect the flames of the fire burning in the open grate, maids
in starched aprons and caps—these are some of the memories
I have of that most comfortable place where Christina
reigned and ruled. The routine and technique of cleanliness
practised and perfected by Christina was a thing to marvel
at. But in the cooking and preparation of the six o'clock
dinner, especially if guests were expected, there was positive
drama.

Figurez-vous, as the French say, the blazing fire, the sirloin
of beef turning on the spit inside a curious tin shelter

hollowed out at the bottom to catch the dripping: Christina, solemn and stern, seizing a long spoon, dipping it in the dripping (which, for some obscure reason, she called "the glory") and pouring it over the roasting meat, which sizzled and spluttered as the spit clicked and turned and went round in the opposite direction. A sort of sacred rite this, with Christina for priestess, and us children, gloating in luscious sounds and smells, for acolytes, sometimes allowed to hold that spoon and pour that rich gravy. Near the fire, stood the shining plate-rack, with its shelves laden with piles of plates and "ashets" of various sizes, all of old ironstone ware, very heavy and of a beautiful pattern. In the background, Forbes, the house-tablemaid, would be busy among trays and glasses, and if there was a dinner-party, Ann's sister Jessie, a professional waitress, would be helping her, passing up and down the kitchen stairs, carrying the glittering silver and crystal, under the watchful eye of Grant, the hired waiter, who was also a confectioner. Not all the grandeur of his evening dress-clothes could take us in. We knew him in his shop, with his apron on, where he became the dispenser of very delectable iced cakes, which he used to hand to us over the counter while Ann was paying the bill.

At the other end of the kitchen passage, looking into the front area, was the laundry. The huge old-fashioned mangle was opposite the window, and there was little else except the long ironing-table under the window, the stove for irons, and, in one corner, a fixed bath with a shower. No one thought of bathrooms in the days when York Place was built; so, when we had passed the age of nursery bathing, downstairs, in dressing-gown and slippers we ran every morning, winter and summer, to plunge into cold water

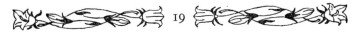

and stand under the cold shower. My father had stern notions of hardihood; but Christina, on very cold mornings, used to temper this Spartan wind to our shivering bodies by lighting the stove, so that we wrapped ourselves in warm towels and dried luxuriously beside the hot little fire.

But it was in washing week that the laundry came into its own. Then the baskets of linen, dried in the sun and air, were brought in, and garments and sheets were wound round the big wooden rollers. Then would the mangle, dead and silent on other days, rattle and clank into life as the handle turned in the vigorous grasp of Forbes or Christina. Back and forth, back and forth it went, hour after hour, and each time its end lifted a roller was pulled out and another pushed in, till all the linen was smoothed and piled ready for the irons next day. That was a good day too, for the stove blazed, and the irons were hot, and ever and anon one would be seized by a strong hand, spat on to test its heat, and, if it sizzled to satisfaction, rubbed on a cloth, then down it would come on the damp shirts and towels and table-linen, and backwards and forwards moved the muscular arms, and the lovely smell of hot clean linen filled the air.

At the top of the kitchen stairs was the long, wide hall, divided into outer and inner hall by an archway. The outer had a hall-table and two stiff chairs and a hat-stand on one side, and on the other stood our big rocking-horse. Rocking-horses are so hedged about with safety devices nowadays that I can't imagine any child caring to ride on them. Now *we* rode dangerously, full of thrills. One of us astride the horse's back, one perched precariously on each rocker, pitching up and down like a ship in stormy seas, we risked our bones in joyous adventure.

The doors of the dining-room and my father's room and the spare room opened on the inner hall, near the main stair-case. The hall was Christina's joy and pride, and great was the quantity of wax and elbow-grease she lavished on the large-patterned linoleum that covered it. How it shone! And so slippery was it, that we must tread delicately for fear of a fall. She resented deeply the muddy feet that had passed by the door-mat without being wiped.

The tall grandfather's clock stood in the inner hall. I can hear the tick of it now. I could hear it from my bed in the nursery, where often o'nights I lay awake, an over-anxious child, listening in fear to the wind howling round the house, and hearing in the lulls the curious whirr that preceded the striking of the hour, and then the strokes themselves, like bells.

The fear of wind dates another far-back memory, so vague as to be more impression than memory: a terrifying tempest, and a late hour; my father coming into the nursery and saying something to Ann, and their voices, almost drowned by the noise of the storm, yet reaching me with the sound in them of horror and distress. That was the night of the Tay Bridge disaster.

THE DINING-ROOM AND THE ROUND TABLE

In my mind there comes another early picture of myself, standing beside Ann and Forbes in the dining-room, while they pointed out its glories to some visitor, I don't remember who. But I do remember the solemn pride in Forbes's tone, and the reverent admiration in that of the visitor. It must have made a deep impression on me.

I knew the room had been freshly "done-up", and was aware that the scheme of decoration was considered to be something rather new, very expensive, and eminently suitable for "the Sheriff's" house. And as that scheme remained during the years I lived in 61 York Place, bearing witness to the first-class workmanship, if rather pretentious taste of those days, I am able to say what it was like.

The walls were panelled in a crimson paper like brocaded velvet, and the panelling, elaborate cornice and high wooden dado were painted to look like oak. I did not think it depressing, I thought it grand. But I do not suppose I ever noticed the real beauty of the room, its spaciousness, its just proportions, the dignity of the two tall windows, the gracious curve of the end wall where the mahogany sideboard stood. The Adam brothers had had a hand in designing some of the York Place houses, so it is just possible that the planning of No. 61 may have owed something to them.

In the windows hung curtains of crimson rep caught up in two long festoons by tasselled cords. In summer these were replaced by Nottingham lace ones, caught up in the same way.

The floor was carpeted up to the walls with something rather dull, which was covered in the centre by a green drugget—ugly, but comfortable, and taken for granted. In the wall opposite the door, in the centre, was the fireplace, with a grey mottled marble mantelpiece. And in the middle of the mantelpiece was the solid black marble clock. It had a beautiful clear face, that clock, with the figures very black and well-spaced, and delicately pencilled, and a pleasant striking tone. How often have I kept an eye on it, as bedtime drew near, hoping that Ann would forget about Louis and me.

At each end of the mantelpiece stood a bronze replica of the horses of St. Mark's, Venice; and there were other small ornaments. I remember a blue china plaque, with, in relief, the white nude figure of Una sitting on the lion.

There were pictures on the walls. On one side of the fireplace hung the portrait in oils of my French grandfather, the Chevalier Nicolas Michel Hallard, a fine rubicund old gentleman in blue coat and white stock, with the red ribbon of the Legion of Honour, and the Cross of the Order of

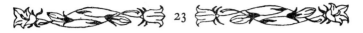

Saint Louis pinned on his left breast. He died at the age of eighty, before my father married.

Many were the stories Aunt Louisa used to tell about her father. He was an émigré, of course, and a Royalist, and had fought on that side.

"Once," said Aunt Louisa, with a face of horror, "in a battle, a great friend of his had his brains blown out, and they were spattered all over your grandfather's coat."

The vision this conjured up of a most unpleasant mess still remains with me.

On the other side of the fireplace, also done in oils, evidently by the same hand, was a picturesque group of heads, those of my French grandmother Elizabeth, very charming, with blue eyes and dark side-curls, and four of her children. One of them, a pretty little rosy child of about three years, became this same Aunt Louisa of my childhood. The other three, two boys, Henri and Alexandre, and the sister Eliza, all died in infancy, and I think lie buried in Normandy. About them too Aunt Louisa had stories to tell.

Eliza seems to have been one of those wonder children who are usually doomed to an early death. We listened with awe to the account of her precocious learning and brilliancy, and of the books she read. I know Homer was one of them.

"Sir Walter Scott," said Aunt Louisa, "was told about her, and was very anxious to see her." But he never did; and she died, poor little girl, at the age of eight, of an illness which Aunt Louisa called "brain-fever". Looking back, I think I must have got the impression that the story of Eliza was a warning not to be too clever.

c

Alexandre also died of brain trouble when he was four or five years old.

"I remember," said Aunt Louisa, "le pauvre petit Alexandre holding his head in his hands and crying out 'O, ma tête, ma tête!'" and then she would clasp her own head with so dramatic a suggestion of pain that I felt an ache at my breast for le pauvre petit Alexandre.

Looking at the little girl's head in the left-hand corner of the picture, which was herself,

"I remember," said Aunt Louisa, "when that was being painted. I remember the studio, high up in a house in George Street, and the smell of paint."

I don't know who the artist was—possibly a pupil of Raeburn.

Among the other pictures, I greatly loved one that hung on the left of the sideboard. I would kneel on a chair and gaze at it with absorbed interest. It was an engraving of one of Noel Paton's pictures, whose works my father much admired, and showed a little boy with long fair hair sitting on a low stool, gazing up, chin in hand, at a huge helmet set on an immense carved chair. Underneath was the title: "I wonder who lived in there!" And I too wondered.

A rocking-chair stood on one side of the fireplace, and a red velvet armchair on the other, beside a small table with a shaded gas-bracket at a level for reading.

There comes to my memory the gracious picture of my father sitting in that chair of an evening, his head, with its cluster of silvery curls, leaning back on the cushion, while he smoked his long pipe, and blew smoke-rings with neat skill for our delight.

ometimes we sat, Louis and I, one on each knee, and

listened in the warm firelight to the old fairy-tales. His voice had magic in it as he led us in imagination through dark forests with Hop o' my Thumb, or to the top of a tall tower, where in our charmed ears rang the cry:

"Sister Anne, Sister Anne, do you see anybody coming?"

As we grew older, and went to school, we prepared our lessons beside him there. I would lean over his shoulder, struggling with my French lesson, while he held the book, and corrected my pronunciation with infinite and affection-ate, if sometimes irritable pains. Ever and anon he would send me to the long bookcase on the other side of the room to look up a word. The French dictionary was very heavy, and I had to lay it on the table; and when I had found what was wanted, I had to put it back in its place at once—a precious discipline in the care of books.

But the chief dignity, the raison d'être of the room, was its centre-piece, the large round table. A round table is a very hospitable thing, to my mind. I can see it now, in the setting of a winter's evening. Warmth, a bright fire, and closed curtains. The cloth has been drawn, as was the custom in those days, and the polished mahogany shines under the lighted chandelier. We have come down for dessert. My brothers are there, and probably Aunt Louisa, sitting opposite my father: Forbes has placed before each the dessert plates of green Wedgwood with the vine-leaf pattern. The glass finger-bowls are on mats having on them charming little hand-painted scenes done in sepia. The cut-glass decanters with claret and sherry stand before my father, and the tall cut-glass jug of water is set before Aunt Louisa. Forbes hands round the roasted chestnuts tucked in a napkin. The high green centre-dish is heaped with red apples.

There is a guest there perhaps. It may be the French cousin Bernay, or the Canadian cousin Ferrier. It may be just one of Harry's friends, D'Arcy Thompson, Monty Macphail, Duncan Robertson, George Gulland, all dear to my father, familiar and kind to us little ones. My father, courteous and debonair, pours the wine, and leads the talk with that polished wit and apt gesture which are his French heritage.

The scene changes to high summer, and in the long night of the north no other light is needed.

Louis and I are a little older and dine with my father and brothers at six o'clock.

The round table has its white damask, shining, different-coloured glasses, and old silver. In the centre the graceful silver épergne, filled maybe with maidenhair fern, is cool and delicate. The meal itself has been simple, suggestive of summer. There has been a salad, of course. In our family the making of a salad was an important business, tackled by my father with joyful skill. There was a gay flourish in the very way he poured the oil, and mixed the vinegar and mustard in the wooden spoon, finishing off by drop-ping a bit of bread touched with garlic into the bowl. To watch him was a delight—a memory to love and to laugh over.

And then the strawberries and cream! There are no straw-berries to equal those grown in the fields of Aberdeenshire, and the scarlet pile glowing in the crystal dish is lusciousness itself.

Who are the guests at this summer table? Madame Davy, my father's friend from early childhood, is almost certainly there, paying one of her long summer visits to us: Aunt

Louisa: Cousin Mary Lees and perhaps Madame Davy's daughter Henriette. Henriette is a very early memory. She did not come often. I know she was pretty and charming and popular, but I greatly disliked her long pointed finger-nails, shaped like the spades in a pack of cards.

Madame Davy was one of the dominant figures of my childhood. Stout, but trim and very upright, she is economically gowned in black with the good taste and perfect neatness of the Frenchwoman. She wears a large muslin bow at her neck, finely tucked, and with bands of narrow black velvet ribbon. The stiff rolls of her white hair made even whiter by powder show in front beneath the smart cap of the period. As we sit there, drinking the vin ordinaire and water, Madame Davy's deep voice rolls out its voluble French like an organ accompaniment to the lighter tones of Cousin Mary's airy mixture of French and English and Aunt Louisa's deprecatory murmurs. Her rich laugh joins with the heartiness of my father's, while her "Ah, Dame!" and the shrug of her broad shoulders are a racy commentary on the talk, itself a gay game, egged on by my father.

Upstairs in the drawing-room afterwards, austere in its early Victorian arrangement of white and gold, mirrors and little tables and white marble mantelpiece, in the pale long-lingering daylight, Madame Davy and Aunt Louisa sit down at the grand piano and play duets. One on each side, Louis and I listen, enthralled, to the overture from "William Tell", holding our breath as the quiet opening moves into the distant mutterings of the storm, and then, as the page is turned, crashes into the thunder and lightning of chords and chromatics, and the two players count and crash and crash and count their way through with grim determination. Aunt Louisa's small hands and nimble fingers rush up and down with never a slip, and Madame Davy's firm fists bring out the stormy octaves in the bass, till once more the page is turned, the tempest dies, and the shepherd's pipe melts our hearts, and at long last comes the finale of gay military music, the last run, the last chord, and the players sink back in their chairs, pleased and panting.

After that Louis and I put the volume of old songs before Aunt Louisa, and find our favourite. "Home they brought her warrior dead", we warble cheerfully but tunefully, and with great emotional relish. Aunt Louisa plays the accompaniment with what we call "expression", looking sentimental and moving her head slowly from side to side in deep appreciation.

Then comes Charlie with his song, "Sir Bertram":

> They shot him on the Ninestane Rigg
> Beside the Headless Cross
> And they left him lying in his blood
> Upon the Moor and Moss.

Oh, how this clutches at my heart, and how Charlie revels in it as he trolls it out with dramatic gusto! And every now and then, unable to resist all this musical stir, Cousin Mary Lees throws in her deep contralto, singing what we call a "second", which excites our warm and envious admiration.

And so goes the summer evening. The long light begins to fade; Cousin Mary Lees thinks it time to say "Good-

night"; Madame Davy sits in the window stitching a new muslin bow, and she and Aunt Louisa talk and talk. Ann puts her head round the door and calls us.

"Bonsoir, mes enfants," comes from the window—and so to bed.

DINNER-PARTIES AND A SUPPER-PARTY

A dinner-party tonight! All day the household has moved in an atmosphere of excited but efficient bustle.

In the drawing-room the red-and-white striped covers have been taken off the sofa and chairs and centre ottoman, revealing them in their ceremonial glory of rose-pink rep. The polishing of the fine steel grate till it looks like silver is to Forbes a labour of love. The beautiful gleam and gloss of the little tables and stiff chairs, on the mirrors and grand piano, is the proud work of her hands. The shining surface of the great mirror opposite the windows reflects the sky, which shows between the rose-pink curtains hanging from their gilded canopies.

Between one window and the mantelpiece is the ebony bookcase, on which stands the bust of my mother, in white marble, by Brodie, backed by a dark blue curtain. Among my earliest recollections is one of my father coming into the nursery of a morning, picking me up in his arms, and carrying me into the drawing-room to "kiss Mamma". Even

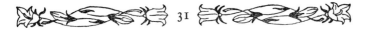

now, after all the long years, I can still feel the cold hardness of the marble against my lips. But even then I thought that marble likeness a lovely thing. I think it lovely now. I could not of course remember my mother, for she died when Louis was born, and I was only sixteen months old. But though I could not remember her, I was never allowed to forget her. I used to hear people say that I was like her, except that my eyes were blue and hers were dark, and I used to look at the marble bust and the picture of her in my father's room and wonder if I was. Her beauty and goodness were Ann's constant theme. People who had known and loved her spoke of her with tears. To grow up in her likeness was to be my high ambition.

The gilt French clock, the sound of its ticking and striking softened under its glass shade, stands in the middle of the white marble mantelpiece, between two little French statuettes of nude female figures, slender and graceful. Water-colours by Perigal hang on the walls, pretty scenes of the Northumbrian countryside to which my mother's people, the Carrs, belonged. On the tables, photograph albums: an ivory box filled with mother-of-pearl counters, engraved with Chinese figures: a china juggler in parti-coloured clothes lying on his back with leg stretched high to hold a candlestick on his foot: and, most admired, most precious, a specimen of Aunt Louisa's extraordinary art, a bunch of paper flowers under a glass shade. The final touch to the preparations is given by the white fur rug in front of the fire. In our eyes that rug is the crowning glory, festivity itself. We would pretend it was the sea, and roll on it with shouts of joy.

Thus the stage is set, waiting for the players.

But I remember how once, on just such an occasion, there occurred a hitch, a crisis, almost a calamity.

Everything, as now, was prepared: the fire blazing: not a speck of dust in any corner: Forbes, always beforehand, ready for the evening, in the whitest and starchiest of aprons and caps. Suddenly, softly, layers of sooty dust began to gather on all the shining surfaces. Horror spread through the house. Up from the kitchen and the savoury smells of cooking flew Christina: out from the nursery rushed Ann with me at her heels.

"Maircy me!" exclaims Ann.

"Losh keep me!" says Christina.

Forbes is leaning out of the window in hot altercation with a sweep, who is standing out in the middle of the street with the end of a rope in his hands: the other end stretched away above our heads towards the roof. What he was doing I never discovered, but that he was to blame for the mess is sure. I have still a clear picture in my mind of that sweep, dirty, defiant, truculent. I remember the deep sympathetic indignation in the voices of Ann and Christina. I remember the new vision of Forbes, having done a lightning change into her working wrapper, re-dusting everything with breathless fury and speed, all the while pouring forth vials of wrathful broad Scots on sweeps and all their sooty ways. I suppose all went well in the end, for I have no recollection of any dinner-party disaster.

We have come in from our afternoon walk, and the party preparations are in full swing. In the dining-room the pleasant and home-like round table has been turned into the long table of ceremony. The long damask tablecloth is brought from the linen-cupboard; Forbes at one end and

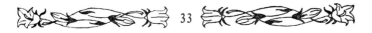

Jessie at the other hold it and unfold it with scrupulous care, so that no wrinkle shall mar the beautiful snowy surface. Their faces are grave with responsibility, for this is but the beginning of things.

Later on Forbes calls me to come and see the completed picture. Now, under the lights, with the curtains drawn and the fire burning brightly, it seems to me a dream of beauty. The serried ranks of forks and spoons gleam and twinkle down the long length of both sides of the table. The glittering galaxy of glasses, pale green, deep ruby and crystal clear, are fairyland. The silver épergne is piled high with bunches of grapes, purple and green: the tall crystal dishes, like lilies on slender stalks, hold crystallised fruits, apricots, cherries, pears: the glass candlesticks, shaped like little lightly-draped boys, hold the tall white candles. Graceful specimen glasses have each a spray of maidenhair fern and one bloom of scarlet geranium—not the real flower, but one of Aunt Louisa's very perfect imitations. The whole effect is formal, but joyous; festive, and very elegant.

Louis and I are dressed and sent in to my father in the drawing-room to await the arrival of the guests. Aunt Louisa is there as hostess, in her black silk dress, the V-shaped opening at the neck fastened with a brooch of garnets.

"Given to me by the Earl and Countess of Wemyss," she would say with pride. Her cap is of white net and lace, with a black velvet bow, and she wears a long gold chain attached to the lovely little watch, set with pearls, which is tucked into her belt. Harry and Charlie are there too. Harry is old enough to be part of the dinner-party.

I have on my new black velvet frock. "Real velvet," says Ann with awe. I know it has cost six pounds and that I am considered to be a most fortunate little girl to possess such a frock. As it is, I am suffering from acute disappointment. I had fancied myself looking like my picture of Mary Queen of Scots. I realise that I do not, and that moreover I feel very stiff and uncomfortable, with a raspy starchy frilling pricking my neck and wrists, at the end of long tight sleeves. Ann called it *mourning* frilling, a name with a most depressing significance.

Mr. Tom McKie is the first guest to arrive. He is some kind of family connection, but is not a favourite with us. He has a slushy method of speech, and waggles his big head in speaking. He has also a trick of saying the wrong thing to a child. He used to bring me presents of cheap chocolate, and waggle his head at me and say:

"Now don't eat it all yourself."

I deeply resented the insinuation, for I was not a greedy child. So now, when I shake hands with him politely, and my father says jocularly, "We have got on our new frock!" he adds insult to the injury of discomfort I already feel by remarking, slushily,

"Ah, but—handsome is as handsome does!" and waggle-waggle goes his head. I am filled with humiliation and rage.

But there are pleasanter guests, and I like the ladies in their soft silks and satins, especially Mrs. Boyd, who wears wonderful broad gold bracelets with fascinating snaps. I squeeze in beside her on the ottoman and show her the photograph albums. Mrs. Boyd is a familiar nursery acquaintance. She is associated in our minds with fabulous wealth, a carriage and pair, and twins called Kitty and Louisa. Ann speaks of them as "the Twinnies". We used to go to parties with the Twinnies and their brothers in the

Melville Street house, in which was a big double drawing-room, where we played with toys that filled us with envy. I remember a model carriage and pair in which we rode ecstatically over the soft and velvety carpets.

Mrs. Herdman is another friendly person. I like her soft Irish voice and accent, and she is the mother of my friend Georgie, with whom I go to tea in Bruntsfield Crescent, which is so far away from York Place across the wide expanse of "the Meadows" and "Bruntsfield Links", that it is like going to spend the day in the country. I also know Mr Herdman's pictures. I have seen them in the Summer Exhibition, to which my father always takes me.

What other guests do I remember? Professor and Mrs. Laurie certainly. I think him very plain, and not very agreeable, but she smiles kindly and I am aware of charm in her manner and in her style of dress, which Aunt Louisa calls "artistic" and means by that a little untidy and unconventional. I chiefly regard her as the mother of Madge, my particular friend, distinctive from my other friends in that she doesn't go to school, but learns lessons with her mother at home. Their home, Nairne Lodge, holds for me some of the happiest memories of my childhood. Madge is always there, with her little dog Prince, full of energy, and full of plans for spending the long and blissful Saturday afternoons. Madge dazzles me by her complete self-possession and precocious wordly wisdom, even though she does not fit into my usual standards, for she can't spell and doesn't learn French, and yet is gaily unabashed and unashamed. I greatly admire her straight-cut yellow hair, which I associate with pictures of medieval pages.

The Blackies do not take much notice of children, but the

Professor, with his long white hair and thin ruddy cheeks, causes a little stir when he comes in. He has an air expectant of admiration. My father delights in him, and we are accustomed to think of him as amusing, but Aunt Louisa pouts and shrugs her shoulders at him and his witticisms. Mrs. Blackie calls him "Hans", a name familiar to me in *Grimm's Fairy Tales*, but sounding strange in my ears as the name of a real person.

I am rather frightened when I shake hands with Professor and Mrs. Fleeming Jenkin. Even grown-up people find them a little alarming at times. He is brightly alert, and his "Well, Nellie?" in that high-pitched voice of his makes me feel shy and ill-at-ease. She is graceful and gracious, but Aunt Louisa thinks her affected. She wears unusual and rather conspicuous gowns—I have the impression that Aunt Louisa doesn't approve of them.

"I remember," she used to tell us, "how once at one of your father's dinner-parties, Professor Blackie was there, and when Mrs. Jenkin came in dressed in one of her remarkable gowns, he was so struck with her appearance that he made her a low bow, and said, 'You are as beautiful as the Queen of Sheba'. And", went on Aunt Louisa, "she held her dress out with both hands, and making him a sweeping curtsey, said, 'And you are as wise as Solomon'."

Of course, we know the Jenkin boys quite well. Austin is Harry's friend, but Frewen and Bernard are just Edinburgh Academy boys, like Charlie and the other boys we know —but they are somehow different from the other boys. Perhaps it is what we called their "English accent" which makes them seem to us superior and aloof. It may be their seriousness, for I don't remember them ever laughing and

joking. And they call their mother "Madam", which sounds to us formal, and very queer.

Little did I realise then how dear and familiar to me that title of hers would become!

"Dinner is served!" says Forbes, throwing wide the door.

Then comes movement and rustle, and the picking up of fans, and polite bows as the gentlemen offer their arms, and lavender-gloved hands are laid on black coat-sleeves. We watch them going downstairs, so gracious, so polite. The soft frou-frou of skirts dies away, and the gently-modulated tones fade into a murmur as the dining-room is reached and the door is shut. Then Ann gathers us into the nursery, and the bright fire with the nightgowns airing on the high fender are pleasant and cheering. Presently there are hurried visitations by Forbes or Jessie, with supper for Ann, and even for Charlie, who sits at the nursery table devouring roast chicken, while Louis and I sit up in our beds and feast on jelly and cream.

I wonder, when I look back, if I am right in thinking that the parties at 61 York Place had in them a certain prestige, some special grace, something above and beyond the customary wide and happy hospitality of those days. If I am right, and I think I am, then that particular quality was due to my father's genial gifts as friend and host. My fancy still brings him before me as a vivid personality, having about him a kind of radiance, which spread itself among his guests, lighting up even the dullest among them.

At the Hellenic Society Supper this personality and radiance must have had full play. That feast of learning joined to luxury took place annually, when the reading of a Greek play was followed by a supper. Sybaritish in its accessories of oysters and good wine and other pleasant things. There must have been a good deal of talking about it beforehand to have given me so strong a sense of its importance.

"The Hellenic Supper," said Ann, "and Professor Blackie will be singin' 'The bonnie Hoose'."

"The Hellenic Supper," said Christina and Forbes, and smiled the tight-lipped smile of the Scot in anticipation of conviviality.

"The Hellenic Supper," said my father, and headed a gay procession down to the cellar, to us the most thrilling of all domestic adventures. The chain clanked, the bolt screeched, the big key, like the key of a stage gaoler, turned in the lock; then the heavy door swung back, and the musty, fusty smell of cork and straw and wine met our delighted nostrils. My father, candle in hand, went from bin to bin, and the glint of light caught the wax seals on the ends of the bottles, red, green and purple, and they twinkled like eyes in the surrounding darkness.

The maids, I think, enjoyed the Hellenic Supper Party even more than the dinner-parties. There was, it is true, less of ceremony and elegance, but the atmosphere of genteel carousal must have been stimulating.

The word "Hellenic" can have meant little to us, and less to Ann. Even so, we all looked forward to something in the nature of a glorious grown-up frolic, which in our imaginations assumed almost Bacchanalian proportions. Not that we had any active part in it, but as listeners, hangers-on in the background so to speak, we managed to get our share in the jollity. We thought it very grand when Charlie was allowed to sit up and even read a part in the Greek play,

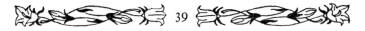

because he was learning Greek at school. But it is likely enough that in Charlie's mind the supper loomed as large as the Greek. Perhaps even in the minds of some of the grown-up members! For though they were, I suppose, a learned crowd, they were of a surety a merry one.

The appointed evening comes. All is made ready, and the house is full of warmth and light. We have to go to bed as usual, but not even Ann expects us to go to sleep, with all the noise of arrival, and the talking and laughing on the stairs, and herself peeping round the nursery door to watch the goings-on.

Who are they all, this intellectual band of brothers and sisters, trooping upstairs, agog for a pleasant evening? I think Professor and Mrs. Sellar would be there, and the Fleeming Jenkins, and certain members of the Bar, who, as Sir Walter Scott has described for us, have ever been ready to mingle larking with learning. I have an impression that Herdman the artist was a member, as I know was Miss Urquhart, a thin elderly lady who lived in Chester Street. I used to be taken to call there, and had heard her speak in praise of Greek, and possibly of suppers.

But the king of the feast, the hero among these Hellenes, is of course John Stuart Blackie, our Professor of Greek, of whom some said, a little maliciously, that he knew more Gaelic than Greek.

Presently all are here, and the sounds of greeting and gossip die as the drawing-room door is shut and the serious business begins. For us there comes a lull, but a lull full of whisperings and comings and goings between kitchen and nursery. They give us some grapes with which we stave off sleep; we are waiting, and the maids listen and wait on the

D

landing. At last the voices of the readers cease, and there comes a burst of talk and merriment as the drawing-room door opens. The play is finished.

Off scurry the maids, and down that jolly company flocks to the dining-room. Now begins the feasting and the fun, as those gay Grecians betake themselves to eating and drinking, and cap the evening with songs and speeches, making the welkin ring with choruses and applause. My father as master of the Revels leads the laughter and proposes the toasts, which are drunk with enthusiasm. Suddenly there is a tremendous clapping of hands. The maids rush up from the kitchen and gather close to the dining-room door, which they open quietly; Ann leans excitedly over the bannister. Professor Blackie is on his feet, and he is going to sing "The bonny Hoose o' Airlie". This is the moment we have been waiting for.

I picture him now, as I have seen him at other times in later days, standing with one arm and hand thrust across his breast, the other free for gesticulation, his head up, the long white hair thrown back:

> It fell on a day, on a bonny simmer's day,
> When the corn grew green and yellow

There is dead silence, while the curiously flat and tuneless voice carries on with the heart-stirring ballad:

> "O, I hae seven braw sons," she said
> "The youngest ne'er saw his daddy,
> But gin I had as many mae
> I'd gie them a' to Charlie."

I was Jacobite to the soul of me, and in that queerly un-
musical rendering there is yet so much of dramatic intensity
that it reaches up to us, alert and listening in our beds, and
holds us spellbound.

Then, oh, then, the joy to us of the storm of cheers and
clapping! The thrill of "For he's a jolly good fellow" and
the "Can you? Can you? Can you?" going round! I thought
they kept saying "Canute", and wondered why that old
king in my History of England should be so constantly
invoked.

More cheers, and then I hear the voices in the hall, the gay
"Good-night"s, the rattle of cabs and carriages driving away.
The front door is shut and the chain fastened. The boys and
my father separate with laughter. Quiet comes back to the
house, the gas is turned out in all the rooms, and we in the
nursery, over-tired, over-excited, at long last fall asleep.

PLAYS, PANTOMIMES AND PLOYS

My first memories of Pantomime are confused but vivid, a phantasmagoria of colours and crowds, processions of Flowers and Jewels, Demons leaping through trap-doors, comic donkeys and talking cats, Transformation Scenes unfolding bit by bit from dimness into bursts of pink and gold glory amid which diaphanous-clad Fairies perch precariously like birds of Paradise, Clown and his tricks, the grace of Harlequin and Columbine and the blunders of Pantaloon, all these flash before my inward eye like first glimpses of Fairyland or the Birth of Dreams.

I am convinced beyond all converting that the Panto-mimes of seventy years ago made a bigger and a better appeal to the hearts of children than they do now. No modern devices, no splendour of electricity can ever persuade me that a series of music-hall turns can make up for no connected story with its pointed moral—Virtue must triumph over Vice, the Fairies over the Dragons, banishing them in the last scene to their own place under the stage

through their own trap-doors—Dick Whittington, Aladdin, the Miller's Son and the Fairy Prince must all deserve their luck and the various villains their fate, or our sense of values would have been outraged. Ballet ladies in pink tights and tarlatan skirts danced but didn't smirk, the hero was ever gallant in trunks and hose and feathered cap, and the heroine dainty in laced bodice and high heels. The realism of bare legs was banned. Our scenery may have creaked, but it was not fantastic; gas flaming through red glass for the Robbers' Cave or through green glass for the Mystic Forest, with limelight to illumine Fairyland may have been primitive, but they lit up for us things magical not merely life-like, which is so dull.

There was a Pantomime of "Aladdin" once, which became a classic in our family. I heard it spoken about and quoted with laughter and appreciation. The "book" was by Sheriff Maitland, my father's friend, and had, I imagine, real literary value and a fine quality of wit. That Pantomime has its place among my earliest memories, as has Pillans the

actor, who played Widow Twankey, and sang, to the tune
of "Yankee Doodle"

> I aince was young and fresh and fair
> But noo I'm auld and yellow,
> Auld Scotland was my native home
> I was born in Portobello.
> I crossed the seas to mairry my Joe,
> Wha'd settled oot in Indy,
> But when I got there I foond he was mairrit,
> So I kicked up a bit o' a shindy.

and kick it she did, with both heels.

The Magician's song has remained with me as the one,
true and only Song for all Magicians.

> My name is Abanazar
> I come from Africa, Sir,
> A first-class Passenger, Sir
> Yo-ho. Yo-ha. Yo-ho.
> Once so merrily hop we   (*he hopped*)
> Twice so merrily hop we   (*higher*)
> Three times so merrily hop we (*higher still!*)
> Yo-ho. Yo-ha. Yo-ho.

And we too hopped, many a time and oft round the nursery
in imitation!

Widow Twankey's other song, to the tune of "Kate
Dalrymple" made warm appeal to my Scottish soul:

> There's a braw braw toon in the far far North,
> O a wunnerfu' toon is our Auld Reekie.

When I sang it—and if I sing it now—I could see, and still see the dim shape of the Castle Rock, the tall grey houses and the smoke above a thousand chimneys.

Charlie was our Theatre "fan", the nursery producer of plays and Pantomimes.

A late Saturday afternoon in winter: we have finished tea and Ann has pulled down the nursery blinds and lit the gas and poked the fire into a blaze. The brass rail of the high fender twinkles. Our shadows grow and lessen on the walls. It is the witching hour. The hour for that life of the spirit in which children live and move to an extent unguessed at by their elders. The corners of the nursery are dark and hold secrets. On the top landing we creep past the dark drawing-room and peep into the empty study where a low fire flickers. One's ear is alert for alarms and whispers. One even courts terror by getting behind a window curtain and shutting out the world. For Charlie this is the hour creative, triumphant. In the twinkling of an eye he is changed from schoolboy to impresario. The space between the windows becomes our stage. A handy arrangement of two poles screwed into heavy discs on the floor supports the cord on which our curtain is hung. Old shawls, tinsel and gold braid (2d. the yard), muslin and spangles, a feather in a hat, toy swords and an Edinburgh Academy blazer, are enough for imagination to clothe all Fairyland and whole legions of Demons. As for scenery, Charlie is ingenious and uses his paintbrush with a flourish. I remember a moonlit sky he made out of a strip of sheeting and painted deep blue. It had a large round hole in the middle hidden by a movable bit of sky, which at a given moment was pulled aside by a completely visible string, revealing Me looking out of the Hole,

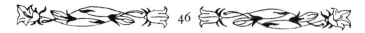

Fairy Moonlight in blue muslin and silver. That blue muslin, all bunch and frills, was made for me by Mrs. Wyndham, whose husband, as far as I knew, was the deity who possessed and ruled over the Theatre Royal itself.

In that blue muslin, I remember standing on our nursery stage, a silver wand in my hand, and singing with much feeling to a big girl called Janie Hay:

> Sunlight we are growing old
> Silver threads among the gold.

The audience, my father and Harry and a friend or two, not to mention the three maids Ann, Christina and Forbes, were appreciative though tickled. The three maids knitted stockings all the time, clicking their needles and cackling with laughter, the clicking and cackling making a running accompaniment in my mind to the acting and singing.

We must have acted "Ali Baba" once, for I remember Janie Hay looking beautiful in my eyes as Morgiana, with her long dark hair and rows of bead necklaces. I felt no dismay at being called upon to take on the parts of First Boy, Leading Lady and Fairy Queen, sometimes at one and the same moment. Charlie of course carried all the principal parts, Ali Baba, Robber Chief, Demon King and the rest on his own resilient shoulders—Louis was the super *par excellence*, representing the boldest of Robber Bands, a host of Eastern slaves, the male chorus and ballet, and all the demons, with a serious competence quite admirable to behold.

The nursery mimings merge into the days when the grown-ups took a hand—a new era. I was between nine and ten years old when the names Gilbert and Sullivan first

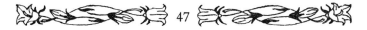

penetrated my consciousness. These two were at the beginning of their collaboration fame.

Charlie was taken to see "H.M.S. Pinafore", then new to Edinburgh audiences. He came home ablaze with enthusiasm, and with ecstatic visions of himself in a cocked hat apostrophising his gallant crew. We must have a Home Production of the opera. His enthusiasm spread from the nursery to the dining-room. "Pinafore" rang in our ears all day. The house was possessed. My father and Ann talked "Pinafore" and discussed difficulties, Charlie shouted "Pinafore" and laughed difficulties to scorn; Aunt Louisa groaned "Pinafore" and prophesied damnation to all concerned, and Harry played all the tunes on his flute.

The scheme took shape, growing, like Jack's Beanstalk, almost in a night. Helpers and cast sprang up like mushrooms after rain. Rehearsals were begun. Dear Mr. Kunz, the husband of my schoolmistress, became for us the kindest, and surely the rotundest, of stage-managers—Maggie Macandrew, a charming person, the thinnest of three very thin sisters who lived with their father at No. 16 York Place, took over the complete orchestra on the drawing-room piano, with Harry doubling the rôles of Conductor and Nightingale (on the flute) in Ralph's recitative.

Clear and dear are the memories of the Saturday evening rehearsals all through the autumn months, when our drawing-room, gay with light and laughter, became an operatic stage, and the music of "Pinafore" made the echoes ring, and the restless movements of young feet shook the long dangles of the crystal chandelier. Here, with my school-friends, Alice and Gertie and Meta, and fourteen-year-old Blanche Kunz (who is to sing off-stage because she is considered too elderly to be on it), are sisters and cousins and aunts in plenty if you count by curls and complacency and not by mere numbers; here in Academy boys is a whole rollicking crew of bluejackets, a round half-dozen of 'em, enough and to spare in all conscience for the manning of a fleet of battleships and ready to stand to their guns all day, and all night too if you give the word. Here we Principals learn our lines and stumble and stick, and Mr. Kunz groups us here and moves us there, and Harry beats time with his flute and tears his hair when double choruses slip the leash and become triple discords, and sailors shout to cousins and aunts and sisters, and cousins shout shrilly back and Maggie Macandrew hammers the keys in vain.

The rehearsal ended, the grown-ups gasp with relief and mop their brows, while we, tireless and free, rush downstairs in a torrent, and set ourselves to the devouring of tongue sandwiches and jam tarts, and almonds and raisins out of the green Wedgwood dish, while Forbes pours mulled claret into the red glasses, to the sound of hilarious chattering. And, almost in a flash, the first performance is upon us, and Friday's school-hours pass with a background of secret excitement. Home from school, there is thrill in the unusual atmosphere of the house and in the appearance of the drawing-room with its rows of chairs and benches and the professional-looking proscenium right across the window end. This has been put up by John, a nursery familiar and odd-job man, a relation of Ann's. He has arranged the oil-lamp footlights, and stands by to draw the curtain. The effective backcloth showing Portsmouth harbour has been painted by Willie Wilson, a delightful person who owned a yacht. He used to take Charlie out

sailing on the Firth of Forth on Saturday afternoons and give him greengage jam for tea.

I am not hungry for five o'clock dinner and have to refuse roast chestnuts. "Bad for the voice," says my father.

Soon we are all gathered in the study, which is our green-room, and has a door opening on to the stage. Dressed for our parts, we gaze at each other in a wild surmise. Bursts of excited whisperings greet each newcomer. I am little Butter-cup, serious though plump, conscious of my little scarlet shawl and dwarfed by Christina's big market basket over my arm. The basket is decked with ribbons and laces. Sisters and cousins and aunts, variously attired, are having rouge added to their noses by Mr. Kunz; Ethel, pertest and prettiest of Cousin Hebes, all gurgles and giggles, flits about in white and blue muslin. Hugo, the First Lord, quite fourteen years, and most divinely tall in my admiring eyes, is magnificent in green velveteen and white silk stockings.

"Hush," whispers Mr. Kunz, as we tiptoe up on to the stage.

"Hush," hisses Harry through a chink in the curtain.

The fateful moment is upon us. We can hear the audience settling in their places. Nervous shivers creep up and down my spine. The opening bars of the overture. We wait, in delicious agony. A bell rings. John draws aside the curtain, revealing as gallant a crew as you could wish, though a bit piratical in appearance perhaps, in striped football jerseys and sailor collars and here and there a fierce moustache. Dick Deadeye, a bearded and sinister ruffian, and most amazingly crooked considering that in real life he is a fine upstanding lad, lurks in his corner. Quite unabashed by the fierce light of publicity beating upon them, the crew start us all off on the ocean blue in a manner that immediately suggests the shiverings of timbers and splicings of main-braces, exceedingly hearty and jolly. The rest of us follow on boldly, and supported by the tuneful turmoil of piano and flute and cheered by laughter and applause we sing and act our way through. Charlie invokes the long-suffering Moon with all the power of his lungs; the Boatswain hoarsely proclaims Ralph Rackstraw to be an out and out Englishman, which he isn't, for Raoul Kunz was born in Edinburgh and his parents came from Alsace. Nevertheless, the chorus vociferously endorses the sentiment, and Josephine, a full head taller than her meek but musical little suitor, comes rushing from the wings to proclaim her love and knocks him, white ducks, straw hat and all, clean into the footlights with a bang.

And so to the end. The last chorus; curtain; roars of applause, bows, and bouquets. Grandpapa, a dear old gentleman, gave me a shilling because he had enjoyed himself so much. He unfortunately died just a week later, so Ann put the shilling in a purse and I was never allowed to spend it.

A year passes, and once more we are in the thick of things theatrical. "Les Cloches de Corneville" is a more ambitious effort, but no difficulties of music or complications of costume daunt our spirits. In the study my father's little desk-lamp with the green glass shade burns late, as he works at the translation of the "Book" from French into easy-flowing English, the English version in use being in his opinion poor and vulgar.

More elaborate care was given to the dressing of the parts for "Les Cloches de Corneville" than for the simpler

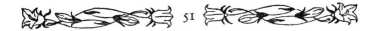

adventure of "Pinafore". "Cranston and Elliot" rose to the occasion. The tall Normandy "coifs" were infinitely becoming to the sisters and cousins of the year before who had added a few to their numbers. Cousin Hebe turned Serpolette was just the jolly little baggage she was meant to be. She had short red hair and a merry laugh, and more cheek than Ann thought at all becoming. Her cider song was full of mischief and sprightliness, and the chorus, following her lead, rollicked along with "Live, good Cider, drink divine" with such wavings of hands and clinkings of glasses that the scene simply scintillated with radiant revelry.

For poor Germaine, who was me, there were no such jolly junketings, for she was the highborn lady, and must behave as such. I have a vivid recollection of an argument between my father and Charlie at the time of the casting of the parts. Charlie was maintaining that Serpolette was the part for me, but I heard my father's decisive "No! My little daughter is to be the lady!" I held my head up, for I felt this to be a noble destiny, albeit perhaps a trifle dull, and was inclined to envy Serpolette having all the jokes to say and getting all the laughs. I had to be serious and ladylike. No frivolity must mar the "Legend of the Bells", however great the temptation in the charming "Ding-dong" chorus. Still, though Germaine could make no bid for laughter, she had an opportunity for what I might call "abandon", in the second act, and a high B flat which always got its guerdon of applause and wreaths. Wreaths? Yes; for those were the days when audiences brought bouquets and wreaths in their white-gloved hands, and threw them to (and sometimes at) the performers at appropriate moments of enthusiasm.

Who would have recognised in the prim little "Bailli",

wearing brown satin breeches and a full-bottomed wig, the once love-lorn Ralph Rackstraw? As for Charlie, the part of Grenicheux, that ne'er-do-weel light-o'-love fitted him like a glove, and in his tasselled Neapolitan cap and crimson sash, with the fisherman's net artistically draped over one shoulder he made as bonny a fisher-lad as you could see in a long day's journey, irresistible to any girl, whether she wore coif or coronet.

But it was Gaspard, the old Miser of Corneville, the erstwhile Dick Deadeye, who was the sensation, the high light, in this dramatic success of ours. He revealed powers of acting that took us all by surprise. Secret guilt, greed of gold, pathos, all were there, and all set out so forcibly that he kept his audience thrilled and enthralled. I shall not easily forget the scene in the château, Gaspard gloating over his guineas (£5 of new halfpennies from the Bank of Scotland), pouring them through his fingers and over his grey-wigged head, and singing his miserly old song about the Chink of Gold, the while Grenicheux shivered with fear behind the splendidly realistic suit of armour. The awful waiting behind the curtain at the back and the sudden clang of the Bells (which hung on straps beside Mr. Kunz, who struck them neatly with a little hammer) which broke the midnight silence, and then the bursting in of the Marquis, me at his elbow, backed by the entire cast, all pointing denunciatory fingers and announcing in strident chorus that they were ghosts; this was to experience one of the crowded hours of glorious life. My heart in my throat I watched Gaspard clutch his gold and tear his wig, saw him stare and stagger and fall senseless, hurling halfpennies in all directions. Then! oh then, did I fling myself on my knees beside him pillowing

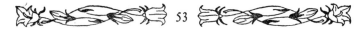

his old head, and stretched imploring hands to the stern and avenging Marquis, while to an accompaniment like muffled drums, I cried in heart-rending recitative, "Good my Lord! Pity this old man!"

Too emotional? Bad for us? Perhaps. But this I know, I would not for a world of puddings and pease be without these poignant memories.

After the last performance there was a supper-party. In our acting dresses, we, the little company, had a table set for ourselves at one end of the dining-room, and the grown-up guests sat at the table of ceremony, my father at the head, the happy host. There was noise; there was hilarious excitement, there were speeches and cheers. I remember the Solicitor-General, Macdonald, afterwards Lord Kingsburgh, trying in momentary lulls to make himself heard. He was a conspicuous person, very big, with a big head and reddish hair, witty and jovial, and keen about things theatrical. What guests besides were there I do not remember, but I know there was a vast deal of merriment.

The feasting done, and when there was a measure of silence, my father rose to speak. Freshly, vividly, I recall the scene. I see my father standing, his hands resting on the end of the table as he leant a little towards his guests whose faces are turned to him in appreciative anticipation. Hushed for the moment, we children are caught up in an atmosphere of tenseness and listening. Child though I was, I was yet aware of a peculiar felicity in my father's diction and choice of words, touching seriousness lightly and lightness with seriousness. Of all he said, much has gone from me, but his finishing words still find an echo in my heart. Looking across to where we sat, a restless excited band, the light of

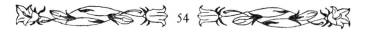

affection in his eyes, a note of deep feeling in his voice, he gave the toast of the evening: "May the Bells of Corneville ring for ever in their ears." Was there one among us who in the years to come could ever hear a strain of the once familiar music without being carried back in thought to those so happy days?

If, as I believe, the theatre and theatrical adventure has a real educative value, then we had it to the full.

I believe that the taste for opera must be acquired early. To a child there is nothing absurd or unnatural in the convention of sung emotions and dialogues or in choral expressions of approval or horror.

To us the trills of the soprano, the top note of the tenor and the bass's deepest note were all a part of this vocal life, a life apart, like life in Fairyland, true with the truth of art and imagination.

My initiation into such a life was through the visits of the Carl Rosa Opera Company to the Theatre Royal. These gave us evenings rich in musical and dramatic experience. More than once I saw and greatly admired Marie Rose as Carmen. Like the music she sang she was sensational and seductive beyond my understanding but not my feeling, and I was fascinated by the exotic grace of her acting and her way of smoking cigarettes. I knew that for ladies to smoke was altogether wrong and shocking, so the spice of the forbidden added to the charm.

Georgina Burns was another of our heroines. She was a notable singer with lungs of steel and a throat of silver. Titania's song in "Mignon" must always be regarded as a tour de force—Georgina's singing of it was a feat in flexibility.

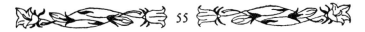

Her name brings back a memory which has tragedy behind it.

The West End of Edinburgh on a still winter evening with darkness setting in. The quiet crescents and streets and the wide-spaced lamps. Suddenly, somewhere, a woman's voice rises, beautiful, resonant, on the frosty air.

The notes fall on the ear with a pathos that hurts. A dark-clad figure stretches a hand for alms and slips away into the gloom.

It was whispered everywhere that this poor bird of the night was the once triumphant Queen of Song, Georgina Burns.

Once a Company doing light opera brought us a performance of "Fra Diavolo". My excitement rose to such a pitch that it was almost unbearable. It led me into a serious lapse. That night I was describing it all to Ann as she brushed my hair for bed. Then with my mind full to bursting with brigands and bandoliers, and my head ringing with tunes and terrors I knelt down to say my prayers. I shut my eyes above my folded hands and saw behind my eyelids none of the ordinary quiet shadows but rampant colours and flaring lights, and instead of the customary "This night when I lie down to sleep" issuing from my usually pious lips, before I was aware I had let out the awful word "Diavolo!" I gasped with horror, but Ann, though a little taken aback, was a person of sense and sympathy. So she tucked me in and bade me sleep in peace. She conveyed the impression that God would quite understand and excuse my mistake. But I never told Aunt Louisa.

I think the first Shakespeare play I ever saw was "As You Like It" at the Theatre Royal. This first glimpse into a

E

wondrous world left me with a vision of a lively but lady-like Rosalind in a doublet which nowadays would be called voluminous, and hose which showed to the knee but no further. She was an actress of some fame and distinction, but her name has gone from me. There were other Shakesperian experiences: Rignold as Henry V waving his sword, his heart-stirring speech before Agincourt marred by painfully asthmatic gasps for breath; the "Merchant of Venice" with Henry Irving and Ellen Terry, a memory of a Jewish gaber-dine on a tall bent figure, whose dark face and darker voice seemed half to hide, half to reveal all the secrets of the East.

As a child, half my life was lived in day-dreams and the source of some of the most enthralling of these were inspired by the play version of Scott's *Rob Roy*, that patriotic perennial, so full of romance, giving vivid and moving expression to that passionate love of the Highlands which has never left me. I myself knew the Pass of Loch Ard, I had picked blaeberries on the Braes of Balquhidder, I had lain among the bracken on the shores of Loch Lomond and paddled in the waters of Vennachar. There was no hero for me like Rob Roy, no tartan but the Macgregor, no traitor like Rashleigh Osbaldistone.

And of a surety Howard was the one and only Rob Roy. What mattered it what the real Rob Roy may have been like? This was he—as we would like him to be. To see him, red-bearded, brooched and bonneted, with skean-dhu and claymore all complete, captured at last and bound with ropes by overwhelming forces of red coats (at least a dozen), having first thrown them in couples about the stage, stand-ing at bay, centre, glaring at his foes, this stirred my very soul with rage and sympathy.

Mrs. Howard, wearing an enormous chieftain's bonnet and the biggest brooches I ever saw on each shoulder, erect on the bridge over the Falls (real water and the noise of splashing) breathing fire through her nostrils as she held her plaid by one hand and thumped it viciously with the other, the while she spat out threats to chop her enemies into as many pieces as there were checks in the tartan, made me hold my breath with delicious terror.

And for weeks thereafter I went my way, walking, playing, doing my lessons, seeing at the back of my mind, myself, a Highland chief, laird of a hundred hills, owner of a Highland castle, living incognito in a town world. I made a tiny wooden sword with a penknife and string, and stuck it in the belt of my pinafore, feeling prepared to do battle with a Lowland host and ready to whistle up my clan. And nobody, not even Ann, had any guess at this secret life of mine.

For Charlie, Rob Roy was simply a gorgeous opportunity. One summer holidays we had a farmhouse at Callander. There was a wide gravel sweep in the front backed by a shrubbery of yews and larches, with a grass clearing just set for a stage. Dear Madame Davy was staying with us. To her came Charlie with six yards of narrow Rob Roy tartan, and demanded that she should therewith and then and there construct six kilts with plaids to match. She held up her hands in dismay.

"Ah Dame! Pas possible!"

However, with many shruggings and protestings, she did his will, turning out six of the scantiest philabegs ever seen in the Highlands.

Undaunted by sparseness of clothing though rather

hampered in their movements by feelings of decency, Charlie as Rob Roy, and five other Academy boys for clan, with me for Helen Macgregor (doubling it with the part of Francis Osbaldistone) and Louis for the depressing Mr. Owen as well as the drunken reprobate singing "Shome shay the Deil's deid" in the last act, gave an outdoor rendering of the play in the little clearing, before an audience sitting round the front door, consisting of a certain Dr. Keith with some fat daughters, who graced the show along with my father and Harry, Madame Davy and the maids. Perhaps Aunt Louisa was there, but it is more likely that she was sitting indoors trying not to look at us out of the window.

Our tiring-room was behind the yews, where the cows in the fields beyond the wire fence watched us while they chewed the cud. There was a yew with spreading branches through which the escaped Rob Roy dashed with magnificent effect on to the grassy stage and nearly on to the heads of his cheering clan. Behind the same yew I perched on a chair, waiting for my moment to appear as the enraged and dauntless Helen. There were red berries on the yew, and there was a pungent smell of greenery.

Private theatricals! Dear half-forgotten phrase, conjuring up the vision of a society which has passed away, taking their standards of behaviour and manners with them. When I was a child, to court publicity was to be vulgar. Charity had not then learnt to advertise, and amateur art needed no money-making scheme for its justification, being regarded as a part of social culture. We acted and played and sang for the pleasure of it, and when people chose to amuse themselves and entertain their friends by play-acting in their own

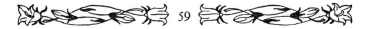

drawing-rooms no newspapermen with notebooks and cameras stood on the doorstep.

Tender memories still cling round the French plays at Madame Kunz's "Private School for the Education of Young Ladies", at which establishment I began my scholastic career when I was yet a very young "young lady" indeed.

These performances were primarily intended for the improvement of the young ladies' French, and this object was kept well to the fore, but I cannot help thinking that it was dear Mr. Kunz's delight in drama, as well as his keen interest in French literature and language, that largely inspired these theatrical events.

He was our stage-manager, and himself wrote little plays for the pupils, all in the approved Alexandrines of the French classics, and all eminently suitable for the most ladylike of young ladies to take part in and still remain ladylike.

One of these plays was "La Table Ronde", with a *dramatis personae* large enough to take in all the boarders and most of the day-pupils besides, for what with King Arthur and his Knights, Guinivere and her ladies, Merlin the Magician and a complete chorus of Druids, there can hardly have been a parent in the audience who could not have recognised with pride and gratification his or her own particular young lady on the stage.

I remember the curtain rose on a forest scene (sufficiently suggested by half a dozen neat green screens) with Druids of all sorts and sizes standing round in a big semicircle. I was the diminutive Druid at one end of the semicircle. We were clad in long white garments of strong cotton, neither mystic nor wonderful, in which we presented an appearance of, I

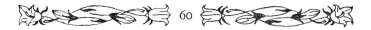

dare say, a rather stolid, and in some cases distinctly solid, angelic choir. At one point we all knelt, and led by the chief Druid, sang an invocation to the sacred mistletoe, addressing it simply and plainly as "O Gui!":

> O Gui! Protége nous
> O Gui! Tu nous vois tous
> Sur les Genoux.

We raised arms of supplication, for the "Gui" was supposed to be up aloft in the pretended branches of imaginary oaks.

Those were the days when for a young lady, in however masculine a rôle, to appear in too obviously male attire would have been considered unseemly, even shocking. Gallant knight or hero for the nonce, she must yet never forget that she was a young lady. I think perhaps that the word "flowing" would have most fitly described the picture of that crowded stage in Madame Kunz's drawing-room. Druids white and flowing, Court Ladies multi-coloured and flowing, Knights in grey sateen armour but still flowing, and head upon head of flowing hair, golden and brown, black as sloes or carroty red. Possibly the French of the young ladies was not always as flowing as it might have been.

But by the time I was seventeen and still at school the conventions must have eased off a trifle, for I remember that in the part of Minet in "Le Chat Botté" I felt not a little bold and brazen in my white fur-trimmed tunic which just reached my knee; but no one was horror-struck. The "Young Lady" was giving place to the "Schoolgirl".

There still be people who remember 3 Great Stuart Street in the days when Professor and Mrs. Fleeming Jenkin lived there. I was much too young then to realise what in

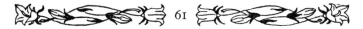

the after days of happy intimacy I came to know, that the years of their stay in that house must have marked an epoch in Edinburgh intellectual Society. Of the two, the Professor remains most vividly in my memory. He had an amazing personality, giving an impression of undismayed optimism. His short slim figure was all alert, and alive. I remember his face, with the side-whiskers and the keen and kindly smile. I think he regarded children with detached amusement, and I was shy and tongue-tied in his presence.

"Madam", the perfect mistress of a house, the hostess whose nimble wit fascinated and at times rather daunted her Scottish guests, was a figure of my childhood whom I regarded from afar, someone I knew but who only knew me as a little girl among other little girls.

The atmosphere of 3 Great Stuart Street awed me. It was so still, so orderly, for all that I knew three boys lived there. The maids were soft-voiced and remote, a little chilling to me, used to the broad smiles and broader Scots of our own three servants.

And yet even in this abode of ordered peace I saw many a transformation to topsy-turveydom in the cause of art, and I was to learn later that the 'perfect mistress' was also a creature of infinite variety, one who, when she so willed, wrought magic.

Far back in the mists of memory I see myself in the dusk of Saturday afternoons all through one winter season delivered up by Ann at the door of 3 Great Stuart Street. I join other children in the dining-room, where already gay groups of grown-up ladies and gentlemen, the ladies in pretty afternoon frocks, are gathering under the lights of the chandeliers. I clutch hold of my particular friend, Madge

Laurie, whom I admire very much although her white stockings are wrinkled and she is always pulling them up. I am wearing bronze dancing-sandals. Lilias Fraser has long curls and a patronising smile. There are boys too, Madge's two brothers Arthur and Malcolm are there. Arthur is elderly, quite fifteen, and I think him very unattractive. Then there are the Jenkin boys and Bob Scott-Skirving and others.

The usually dignified room, fit for grave academic feastings, has been changed as by Harlequin's wand to a hall of revels, carpet rolled up, table vanished, chairs set round the walls, while in a warm corner by the fire sits a white-haired, white-bearded old fiddler tuning up the strings of his violin. At the far end near the windows Madam is marshalling her laughing guests into "sets", and the ladies are holding their skirts high above the ankle as they practise their steps. On the sideboard sits the Professor, legs dangling as he smiles at us children chattering and jostling ourselves into our places for the dance. We little girls are quick to snatch at the partners of our choice before they can evade us. George Cunningham is a chief favourite. He must be at least twelve years old, a hero in a blue serge suit, with beautiful dark eyes and charming manners. There is nothing about the Scottish reel in all its variations that the Professor does not know, and his Celtic fervour is all alight to guide and direct us through all its intricacies. His enthusiasm is infectious, and we are ready, one and all, to do or die.

I hold out my short frilly skirt and place my feet in the fifth position—Mr. D'Egville, the dancing-master at school, has taught me that. The old fiddler scrapes out a chord, then breaks into a stirring Strathspey. Off we go, slide, together, step, hop, round and round in the figure-of-eight, set to partners and round again. Presently the rhythm changes, and the wild music of the Reel of Tulloch sets us a-whirling, and the beat of the quick-step drums on the floor. Soon we are panting for breath, but our feet do not falter. Swing and step, swing and step, and now and then a wild whoop from some particularly Highland-minded male dancer, till the fiddler stops at last on a harsh chord bringing us up with a jerk. There are gasps of relief, much laughter and the clapping of hands, and the dancers swarm into the hall for coolness and into the library for tea. There are short intervals between reel and reel, and in every interval you might see three little girls, Madge and Lilias and me, seated at a round table in the tea-room, elegantly drinking tea out of elegant cups, and eating slice after slice of the very thinnest of thin bread and butter, and all the time our tongues wagged making polite conversation. Says Madge, between bites:

"My father is a Professor in the University."

"My papa is a Sheriff," say I, not to be outdone.

Lilias tosses her head with what Madge and I consider a very affected air.

"*My* papa," she says, "is Lord Advocate."

Madge is never abashed, but *I* think Lilias proud and disagreeable.

Reels may have little to do with plays or play-acting, but they serve to introduce the attitude of that orderly house towards unusual and interesting doings. Also, the Professor on the sideboard was not the mere Teacher. He was the inspired Producer.

For it was the private theatricals of 3 Great Stuart Street that made that house memorable to many people.

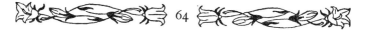

Among her many and divers gifts "Madam's" gift for acting was supreme. It was therefore a most happy circumstance that the Professor, with a keenly critical appreciation of acting, had also a genius for stage-management. The combination of these two remarkable people, aided and abetted by a group of talented enthusiasts, brought about great achievements in amateur dramatic art.

My childish impressions surround these theatricals with an aura of glory. It may well have been that it was in those early days I first became dimly aware of the tremendousness of Greek Tragedy.

I can recall in part the setting and something of the atmosphere of the Greek plays. I seem to see at the back of the stage a step and a white archway. Is it "Clytemnestra" who appears there, a Greek statue come to life? She steps down, coming slowly down stage, her every movement and the expression of her face sombre, ominous with the suggestion of inevitable fate. I remember no words, but the tones of her voice, resonant with apprehension of horror to come, hold her audience spellbound, and the appeal of her outstretched arms is unforgettable.

But there was Shakespeare as well as Sophocles or Aeschylus—"Antony and Cleopatra" brings some clear pictures to my mind. I must have been about ten when I sat on an end seat among an audience which filled every corner of that long dining-room, and craned my neck to watch the crowded scene. It was perhaps no case for wonder that a child's taste was better pleased with such a play, so full of movement and colour, than with the austerity of Greek drama. And besides, in this production of "Antony and Cleopatra" I had a secret and exciting interest. Charlie had

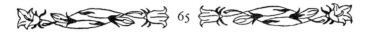

been chosen for the part of "Boy with Song", and while I watched the stage I waited anxiously for the moment when Antony, played I think by Mr. Hole the artist, seized Charlie by the arm and mounted him on a stool saying "Sing, Boy!" Trumpets blared out the first bars of the tune, and Charlie, in tunic and Roman boots, his dark curly hair wreathed with vine-leaves, a golden goblet in his hand, trolled out, in his ringing boyish voice, that roystering ditty:

> Come, thou monarch of the vine
> Plumpy Bacchus with pink eyne.

I never saw the music of that song, or ever heard it again, but I can sing every note of it.

One other scene of that play comes freshly before me— "Cleopatra" and her maidens, the countryman and his basket, its dire freight hidden in leaves—I laughed at that countryman and his talk about "the worm", but I heard "Cleopatra" cry "O Antony!" and so I watched, hushed and awed, for the coming of the end.

But Comedy follows quick on the heels of Tragedy. Our eyes, wet with the sorrows of Clytemnestra or Cleopatra, are hardly dried before the fun of the Merry Wives and Falstaff fills them with tears of laughter.

"Here comes the big fat man again!" calls out a delighted small boy, and we shout with joy as Falstaff comes rolling on to the stage, the twinkle in his eye, his stick in his hand. And the two Merry Wives peep out from the corners and laugh and laugh with their hands to their sides, and their two tall caps bob and nod at each other as mischievously as you please.

Or it may be Mrs. Malaprop who sails on to the stage

crinolined and befrilled, the expressive fan in her hand, the brave wrong words on her lips. Could this again be "Madam", who had so lately wrung our hearts? Ripples of laughter greet her every pompous pronouncement. Learned progenies and headstrong allegories come rolling off her tongue, unerring in wit and emphasis.

I turn another page of memory. This time the curtain rises on a scene where my thrilled eyes recognise Frewen and Bernard Jenkin as the boy and girl who rock a cradle and sing "hush-a-bye baby" as they rock. The little elderly man in shabby knee-breeches is the Professor, this time actor as well as producer. To them enters Peg Woffington, "Madam" herself, Fairy Godmother to this poor family, and with her come joy and plenty. At her command the little negro boy stands in the doorway, holding high a huge dish filled with a huge pie. And even with his face as black as a boot I know him at once, for my handsome partner in the reels, George Cunningham. Then oh! the rollicking glee of the Irish jig, as Peg kilts her skirts and kicks her heels with the lightness of down, and Bernard foots it gaily beside her, and the Professor leans up against the wall, his face all smiles, fiddling like mad on a dumb fiddle while off stage and unseen, our old fiddler of the reels plays the tune.

Memories or impressions? I cannot be sure. But, of a surety, those were the days!

AN EDINBURGH SUNDAY IN THE '80's

One awoke on Sunday morning to a city of silence. No sound in the streets of trams or carts, and no cries of coalmen. The rare rattle of a cab and the clip-clop of the horse's feet on the stones have an ungodly ring. For to drive in a cab on Sunday, except in a case of "needcessity", as Ann would say, was to break the Sabbath, and to break the Sabbath was to imperil the soul, *and* to pay double fare into the bargain, and I really don't know which we in Scotland considered the worse penalty of the two.

No sweet chimes usher in the morn as in lighter-minded lands. Early church-goers, Catholic or "English Church", must walk in quietness. Not till the forenoon is well advanced, when every steeple and tower will set harsh bells a-clanging, must there be any disturbance of the Presbyterian Peace.

The signs of Sunday are all about me as I run downstairs, dressed in my Sunday frock. The shine and polish of yesterday, but no bustle of today. I hear Forbes in the kitchen grinding the coffee-beans in the little coffee-mill. The beans make a scrunchy sound and the smell is delicious.

The round table in the dining-room is laid for breakfast and the big brass kettle is beginning to sing on its gas ring attached by rubber piping to one of the jets of the chandelier. My father has cleared a space for the enormous fat family Bible and found his place. The first bell is rung, for prayers. The second bell will mean breakfast. On week-days there is a third bell, for porridge, between prayers and break-fast proper. Very confusing for the stranger within our gates.

Forbes and Christina come in and sit near the door in their clean prints and aprons, their hands folded primly in their laps, their fine thin Scottish faces models of Sabbath solemnity. Ann slips unobtrusively into a corner and shakes her head at Louis and me as a warning to behave properly. If Aunt Louisa is there, she sits in the velvet armchair, her mouth drawn down, her face grim with disapproval of my father's method of reading the psalms and prayers, which is scholarly but breezy. When we say the Lord's Prayer she does her protesting best to slow down the pace, and caps my father's cheerful "A-men" with an evangelically emphatic "*Ay*-men", and I feel quite sure that "*Ay*-men" is more religious than "A-men".

No emotional memory of family prayers stirs in me. But one picture remains of a happening brought about by our custom of the three bells.

A morning in summer when Madame Davy was our guest. She was a Catholic, so did not come in to prayers, and being French she was not expected to like Scotch porridge.

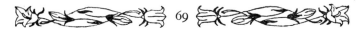

So she had been bidden to wait until the third bell had sounded before joining us in the dining-room. But this morning she must have forgotten which bell meant which. My father had finished the psalm and shut the Bible with his characteristic gesture of decision, not to say with a bang, at which signal we all with one accord turned our backs on him and knelt down. I counted the buttons on the leather padding of the chairs the while I let the words of the General Confession creep in my ears. Suddenly I heard the door open, and turned my head to see Madame Davy standing there irresolute, startled by this unusual and peculiar back-view of the household.

Now I knew all about Roman Catholics from Aunt Louisa, and conceived of them as a people plunged in the darkness of superstition. What would Madame Davy do? Would she turn and flee as from mortal sin, or would she stay and risk damnation? I watched, fascinated. And then I saw her close the door softly and kneel down, in her black gown and her wondrous snow-white coiffure, and with bent head and meek devotion join in our Protestant prayers. My childish mind, imbued with prejudice, took a leap forward, and I saw a new vision of understanding and tolerance.

"A-men," says my father; "*Ay*-men," comes Aunt Louisa's stern correction. And up we all spring. My father makes the coffee in the "Napier" machine, to my mind, the cleverest and prettiest of all coffee-making devices. Forbes brings in the hot muffins, English muffins, a new bakery venture of "Mackie's" perhaps, and a new luxury on our Sunday breakfast-table. Christina scorns them even while she serves them. She knows well that all the muffins in England cannot compare with her scones, especially her

triumph of triumphs, the "soople" scone. This is not so much a scone as a World's Wonder. Flattened to a wafer-like thinness, buttered with lavishness, tenderly rolled, it is devoured lusciously, the butter oozing out at each end, and vanishes like a succulent dream.

When I was a child there was no talk of making Sunday a happy day for children—children had just to try to be happy though Sunday. Aunt Louisa said all good children loved Sunday better than all the other days of the week. I knew that. All my story-books were full of such children, like Marianne in *Anna Ross, the Orphan of Waterloo*, who was converted by Anna and almost immediately died, words of piety on her lips and forgiving all her relations. I realised that Marianne was a pattern, but I didn't want to be as good as all that. I think our half-conscious feeling about Sunday was that it was the waste of a perfectly good day which, under happier auspices and more skilful planning, might have been another Saturday. But we knew there was no getting past that first chapter in Genesis, so we accepted things as they were, thankful for alleviations, like coffee for breakfast, and that at least it wasn't another Monday. But it was certainly a day of bans and restrictions. The toy cupboard must not be opened, my dolls must lie abed. It was accounted sin to be seen with a needle in your hand. There must be no music, except what was called "sacred"; no singing unless hymns; and as for whistling, if one of the boys so far forgot himself, or the day, as to let forth one solitary trill, down in the lower regions Christina heard, and rushed, a thin little creature all fire and fury, up the kitchen stairs, and breathless with horror,

"Laddie!" she gasps out, "d'ye no' ken it's the Sawbath?

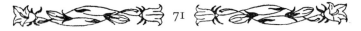

An' a' the folks is stannin' in the street lookin' up at the windeys!"

To affront the neighbours—that, for Christina, is sin unpardonable.

Possibly we, as a family, were less oppressed by Sunday obligations and observances than some of our friends. The French blood in our veins militated against gloom, and being Episcopalians a certain laxity was almost expected of us. In kindly phrase, we "knew no better".

We went to church at St. Paul's opposite—oblong, ornamented with rows of little pinnacles and spikes, with a short round tower at each corner, it provoked the scorn of Aunt Louisa.

"Just like a table turned upside down," she said. But then she considered St. Paul's "high", and herself attended St. Vincent's, an insignificant little chapel with a type of service almost belligerently low.

The bell of St. Paul's begins its cracked and toneless clanging. There is still plenty of time for us to stand at the dining-room windows and watch the congregation gathering. This is the maids' hour of hours. They counted it as glory that we lived in a house with a church so handily placed. Peeping out, hidden by the curtains, they would watch the world go by to public worship. The assembling and "skailing" of congregations was their weekly panorama. To be thus the secret audience of the godly had for them the tang of dissipation.

I have a dim memory of my brother Harry standing beside me at the window one Sunday. I knew he was keeping a look-out for "Maude". My father laughed, but I was jealous. I caught Harry's sentimental murmurings about

F

Maude's beautiful long hair, and I hated Maude, for Ann did my hair in tight curls which she brushed round a porridge-stick every morning.

My whole interest is centred in the little "Cargilfield" schoolboys. They come hurrying round the corner of Broughton Street in little chattering groups, and I stand and gaze, adoring them in their Eton suits and little top-hats, each with a huge unrolled umbrella as tall as himself. I wish passionately that Louis wore an Eton suit, a garb that he as passionately scorned.

When the cracked bell begins a series of excited jangles and the last stragglers come swooping like frightened birds from all directions and in at the churchyard gates, we issue forth with dignity and cross the street at leisure, feeling superior to the hurrying hordes. I glance round and catch Ann still at the window watching us. She takes a proprietory interest in us all, but me she regards with an artist's eye, as being from my hat to my heels the work of her hands. My curls, like glossy sausages, hateful to me, are her peculiar pride and care; my black button boots shine; not a wrinkle shows in my ribbed white cotton stockings. Perhaps I have on my new frock, pale grey with little pleats. I am very proud of it, for it has been made for me at Maclaren's in the High Street instead of by Ann's niece, who was a dress-maker with no imagination. My hat is a pale lemon-coloured straw, scuttle-shaped, and the palest of pale blue neckties is tied under my chin. But alas for Vanity! "It's all too colour-less," said my Father impatiently, when Ann proudly set me before him for approval. Dashed but undaunted, Ann rose to the occasion. She flew, she fetched my coral necklace and clasped it round my neck below the necktie; to set that off

she added a silver chain below the necklace; then capped the colour scheme with a second coral necklace below the chain —my father was satisfied.

Frocks: visions of them, Sunday frocks, party frocks, school frocks, from the days of starchy white pique with frills and a Roman sash, and a hideous garment called a "polonaise", from my lilac poplin with black velvet bands stitched across my front like the bars of a grate, on to the time of the prettier Princess fashion—these flash before my inward eye, marking the years, and holding for me memories of pride and bitterness, satisfaction and disappointment. One is so helplessly dependent on the taste of one's elders. One may exclaim and wriggle at tightness and starchiness, but it is a struggle against inexorable fate.

Ann's taste in frocks might be described as a mixture of love and thrift. Nothing was too good for me, but everything must be let-downable or add-onable, so that all my garments started by being too long and too loose, and just as they got to be comfortable they were lengthened and loosened. In my nursery days frocks for little girls were apt to be modelled on grown-up styles. I have a photograph of myself at about the age of eight, in a garment which had a separate little bodice (called by Ann my "body") shaped to my small shapeless figure and buttoned with many buttons down my short front. It was vivid purple, and I hated it.

But Ann's real passion in dress was mourning. No one whom I ever knew had a more feeling heart, but I think for her, as for most Scots, death shed a lustre on life and she found consolation in the "trappings and the suits of woe".

My grandfather died when I was nine, and I was at once

clothed in black cashmere, so lavishly trimmed about with crêpe that I must have looked like a miniature widow of that period without the cap. So clad, I was not myself unaware of the aura of melancholy glory which surrounded me.

We enter St. Paul's by the west door and climb the stairs to the south gallery. A respectable but grim old person in a black bonnet shows us into our front pew, and stands like a gaoler, counting heads, till we are all safely in, and after placing a large prayer-book and the collecting bag on the bookrest before my father, she shuts the door with a snap, shooting the bolt home, and leaves us to settle ourselves among the red baize cushions and footstools. There were galleries round three sides of the church, and all the front pews were upholstered in red baize, which gave one a comfortable sense of sumptuousness combined with unctuousness, and which was felt to be handsome and proper for people like us. Humbler folk in the pews behind had just to make do with plain polished wood.

The gallery on our left, which faced the chancel, sloped up to the high organ-loft where the choir sat. Two rows of stone pillars, fat and fluted, hemmed in and partly supported the galleries. They obstructed one's view sideways, making the pew alongside ours ever for me a tantalising mystery. But one forgave them that on Christmas Day. On that one day of all the year gaiety came to St. Paul's, and our eyes were gladdened with greenery lighting up greyness. On that one day every pillar was wreathed about with holly, while the choir, sitting far aloft like the angels, sang "Christians awake" across a perfect barricade of berries. On that one day the high pulpit fairly rollicked in scarlet and prickles, looking like some strange Christmas tree, out of

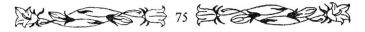

which Dean Montgomery in his black cassock stuck up like a Demon of Darkness caught unawares.

There was a time when I had to stand on a footstool to peer over the padded bookrest to see the congregation on the floor of the church. The little Cargilfield boys sat on a long bench running lengthways down the north aisle. During the prayers they turned and knelt on the hard tiles, and their legs stretched across the aisle, so that a latecomer had to perform a kind of tiptoe hurdle race to get to his front pew. The legs were clothed in grey trousers and the Eton jackets were very short, and that long row of little grey behinds must have been an inspiring sight.

The eleven o'clock service was very long. So was the Dean. So were his sermons. One sought distraction. In our pew there seemed to be an endless number of prayer-books and hymn-books of different shapes and sizes. One Sunday during the Litany I collected a quantity of these and laid them out on the red baize bookrest in front of me, arranging them in a beautiful mosaic pattern, taking great pains to fit the corners in neatly. Suddenly I glanced up and saw the ladies in the choir looking down at me with smiles. I was terribly ashamed, and immediately sank down out of sight among the footstools. I regarded the choir-ladies ever after with suspicion. I thought them very plain, and the choir-men plainer. They sat behind the ladies on each side of the organ and sucked lozenges. There was a long thin dark one who sang bass, and stretched his chin to reach the low notes. And there was a fair fat one who looked as if he could bellow but sang a weak tenor and had a pained expression as if singing hurt him. I could see the back and shoulders of Mr. Jamieson the organist, and sometimes his hands on the top manual. But my real interest was in his two pale-faced, black-haired little sons in velvet suits, who stood one on each side of their father and pulled out the stops. This seemed to me to be a post of supreme glory, and I regarded them with awe.

Another distraction was the La Cour family. They sat in the opposite gallery, in a pew like ours only nearer the chancel and overlooking the pulpit, to my mind then a most enviable situation. There was a whole row of La Cours, father and mother and quantities of little girls with blue eyes and flaxen curls. I found them of absorbing interest and beautiful as the children of my dreams. I can remember how, as the years passed and the first crop of little girls grew into big girls and lost their pristine fairness, there always seemed to be another crop as flaxen as the first crowding up the pew. When I was about eleven and went to Sunday school, I got to know the elder group, Constance, Mabel, Ethel and Mildred. No longer the children of my dreams, they still intrigued me. They were so overpoweringly churchy, and so easily shocked. They rattled off the collect with annoying fluency, and bowed their heads in the creed. Not so much a bow perhaps as a jerky familiar little nod. I, self-conscious and thoughtful, could only wonder at and admire this easy intimacy with things of the spirit.

St. Paul's Church: how memories of it cling, and come crowding into my mind! The Children's Service, in the days of Dean Montgomery was a most cheerful occasion, when the Cargilfield little boys were for the nonce transformed into a jolly angelic choir and sat in the gallery below the organ, row upon row of curly heads and Eton collars, all ready to lead the singing. And lead they did, with a

vengeance, and we followed with such stupendous results in the way of treble blasts of sound that the two Jamieson boys were kept busy pulling out all the loudest stops to give the organ a chance. It was a glorious hour, all our young lungs at full stretch. With what gusto did we proclaim that there was a Happy Land far far away! How joyously we shouted encouragement to one another to work for the night was coming! And when it came to pitching our moving tent a day's march nearer home, not even a circus tent could have withstood the hurricane of breath that blew among the pillars.

A year or two later the old Dean was transferred to the new Cathedral in the West End, and Mr. Ridgeway came to us in his stead. Then new life stirred among the dry old bones, and a brighter light illumined the dark corners of that most respectable and conservative place of worship, St. Paul's Church.

As a congregation we were a little stiff to move at first. We were startled when Mr. Ridgeway preached in his surplice, a daring innovation, savouring of Popery. But there was no doubt it brightened up the pulpit. Then he suggested that we should stand when the clergy entered the church, arguing that it was simply a piece of good manners. That was a shock. We shivered, but survived, and obeyed. But Aunt Louisa was horrified.

"Oh," she cried with fierceness, "if only old Bishop Terrot were alive! I know what *he* would have said!"

I waited to hear. Aunt Louisa pushed me down on the nearest chair.

"*This*," she hissed. "Sit *down*! There's a Higher Presence here."

I resented Bishop Terrot. He was dead anyway, and I could see no reason why a High Presence should object to good manners.

And so we all came alive under the new régime at St. Paul's, and sang "Onward Christian Soldiers" at the Children's Service instead of the singularly inappropriate "For ever with the Lord", and Louis and I played in the Queen Street gardens with Una and Gerald Ridgeway, and when Gerald became a Cargilfield boy I swelled with pride because I actually knew a boy in an Eton suit.

Church-going had for us its moments of drama. One of these occurred every time the Athanasian Creed was appointed to be said or sung. My father strongly disapproved of Athanasius and his drastic doctrines, and whenever the choir began "Whosoever will" bang went his prayer-book, and down he sat in his corner, his arms crossed in defiance, and the expression on his face so sternly scornful that I feel sure the Saint himself would have quailed before him and gone straight home to bring out a revised edition. We had to sit down too of course, feeling conspicuous. Still, it had something of daring and adventure in it; to sit square, so to speak, before the hostile forces of clergy and congregation, not to mention choir. There was something about our attitude of the bloody but unbowed which I feel sure must have shocked the La Cour family very much.

Then there was the Collection. Here was Drama, touched with Glory! It was grandeur beyond telling to have a father who took round the bag, first putting in his own contribution. I have seen him on special occasions thrust in a crackling one-pound note, and have felt in my own person all the glow of a reckless generosity. When he joined the

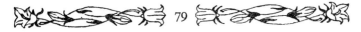

other collectors downstairs I would stand on a stool to watch the procession of black-coated elderly gentlemen march up the aisle to slow music, and "there's Papa" I would say to myself, and hoped the La Cours saw and admired and envied.

One other church moment I must speak of. One which ended for me, when I was thirteen, on a note of sombre tragedy. When a member of the congregation died, Mr. Jamieson used to play the Dead March in "Saul" at the end of the service. As I remember, neither clergy nor congregation stayed to hear it, but filed out as usual. But the choir waited, and we waited, standing in our pew, gravely thrilled, till the last roll of drums had died away. Three days after my thirteenth birthday I stood again to hear the Dead March played, but this time down below in the centre of the church, with Ann and Aunt Louisa standing on either hand. I was cold and dry-eyed among many who wept. Suddenly from the far organ-loft behind me came the first shuddering roll of muffled drums. The Dead March. In a flash I saw again my father in our gallery pew, conspicuous in the beauty and dignity of his silver hair, as he paid reverent tribute to the dead. And as they led me down the aisle behind his coffin heaped with flowers, I broke into a passion of uncontrollable tears.

We would come in from church to find the table set for lunch. A small cloth covered one end, on it tumblers and wine-glasses on a tray, the decanter of sherry, water in what Forbes called the "carafe", cheese, and biscuits in the silver biscuit-box. That great function of the South, Sunday Midday Dinner, was to us a feast unknown. On the Sabbath Day in Scotland we fared, rich and poor alike, with a

Spartan-like simplicity. Water biscuits are not appetising eating for a child, so we didn't eat and nobody bothered.

In the afternoon we always went to call on Grandmamma. Grandmamma lived on the south side, in Blacket Place. That meant a long walk, made longer but far more interesting by taking the way of the Queen's Park. After passing through the Gate at Holyrood we sometimes turned right, and climbed up to the Weavers' Walk, wending our way along that high precarious path below the Salisbury Crags, where the edge fell away so steeply that my father would clutch nervously at Louis and me as we peered over to see a loosened stone go with leaps and bounds down to its final crash at the bottom.

At the top, just where the path begins to slope away down on the other side, we would stop to draw breath and look across to the grey city in its smoky haze, and in its midst the Castle, that misty watch-tower of the North, grim, yet benign. We would sit and rest in the shelter of those rugged rocks, where the "Cat's Nick" tempted the adventurous to climb a hazardous way to the summit. The Queen's Drive, far below us, wound away to the left and up towards the "Windy Gowl" (gully). Behind the Crags, in a hollow of the hill, lay "Hunter's Bog". And as we rested my father would tell again the story of the French weavers who years ago came and settled on a bit of land between Edinburgh and Leith, familiar to us now as a street called, after them, Picardy Place. In those days, the citizen travelling eastwards could hear, while still afar off, the sound of their looms, busy and prosperous. But the evil days of the Industrial Revolution came upon them and they were caught up in calamity, and were near to starving in a strange land. At which time the

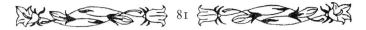

good town of Edinburgh, being moved by pity, bestirred herself and found work for their hands. And thus was built, and, as I think, as much to the Glory of God as any Cathedral, this wonder walk along the steep hillside. Up here there is a fine remoteness, a Highland wildness. Here at times is heard the calling of gulls as they hover and scream over St. Margaret's Loch. Here too the easterly haar, blown in from the sea, sweeps across like smoke, wiping out the world below, while the crags above loom through a ghostly blanket. Here are wide skies and the thrill of the wind in your face. I cannot forget that Weavers' Walk, and I feel that I owe something, something intangible but real, as do all who have a love for heights and depths, rough tracks and far horizons, to these poor people of Picardy.

Sometimes, leaving Holyrood behind us, we would turn to the left after entering the Park, and pick our way along the shore of St. Margaret's Loch, blue and sparkling in summer sunshine. We would scramble up the rough track to St. Anthony's Well, which bubbles up a long way below the ruined Chapel of the Saint. Much weary trailing must he have done, that poor creature of temptation, down over the grass and boulders, and up again with his brimming pitcher. But I cared nothing about him as I drank easily from my cupped hand, wishing, as was the custom at the Well, many a long-forgotten wish.

On and up, winding along the eastern slopes of Arthur's Seat, following no path, but finding ways among the golden whin-bushes with their honey smell, where the blue-bells grew, and the larks rose startled into the high sky. Before us the sheep scattered, bleating at us from the green shoulder of the hill which stretched up and up on our right hand. What child could pace sedately among such tempting beauties? I picked bluebells, and hoped against hope they would not fade this time; I pushed my face down among the yellow gorse to get a closer smell of it, pricking my nose most viciously. I hid among the whins, in some tiny clearing, in a minute-long pretence of solitude, letting the others pass by unseeing, then rushing after them in sudden fear of being really left alone.

Charlie, far behind us, lingered and dawdled, looking out for butterflies. He collected butterflies, and I think walked in hope of spying some new strange winged creature flit across his path. But, as I remember, only the little blue ones haunted this hillside.

These were the nearer joys; but to stop and look further afield, to take in that incomparable sweep of sea and islands and distant hills, was to court an enchantment that has stayed with me, becoming ever "more endeared" with the passing of the years. With my hand in my father's I looked across the blue Forth to the Lomonds of Fife. Inchkeith and the Bass Rock seemed close and familiar, but the dim shape of the far-away "May" was like the Island of a Dream.

Amid scents of honey and wild thyme, and the soft sea-wind blowing, we come down again to the road beside Dunsappie, grey and deep in the shadow of the hill, and presently see below us the gleam of a wide water, which is Duddingston Loch, beautiful in its setting of tall reeds. On a rocky promontory the little stone church stands, the guardian shrine. The swans float near the shore, watching for passers-by, hopeful of a scattered largesse of bread.

Sunday and the summer fade before a vision—Duddingston Loch in winter. A clear day of keen frost, a red sun, a

sheet of ice, and snow on the hill. In one's ears the throbbing hum of skates skimming on thick ice. Thousands of skaters, and among them Me, a small girl in winter coat and a beaver hat with scarlet ribbon, perched dangerously but gloriously on a pair of strapped skates, clinging, breathless with joy and fear, to some experienced hand.

A few years, and again I see myself, a schoolgirl of fifteen, moving now with easy confidence, hand in hand with Madge Laurie and her brother Arthur, laughing, chattering, gliding round and round that great expanse, endlessly, excited with the splendour of the keen air and the swift going. How stiff we are, but how jubilant, as we walk, a merry group, skates jingling, back through Duddingston village and the frosty dusk to the Lauries' home, that house of many memories, Nairne Lodge. The stone-flagged Hall, its shabby Eastern rugs lit up by the blazing fire, gives us welcome. Upstairs in the drawing-room Heaven awaits us in the shape of hot buttered toast and Kitty pouring out tea and gay talk round a warm hearth.

These mind pictures come crowding, interrupting, crossing one another. I have to seize them as I can, ere they pass.

After the freedom and adventure of the walk by Arthur's Seat, to enter through the gates which shut off Blacket Place from Dalkeith Road was enough to strike a chill to every childish heart. The gates were never closed, but they seemed to us a symbol of cold exclusiveness, and of an infinite dullness. The long curving row of square-built houses, each with its tidy front garden and iron railings press down like a weight on our spirits. I had to be much older before I could appreciate the austere charm of the grey stone and the formal gaiety of beds of scarlet geraniums, mixed with the yellow of calceolarias, and bordered by blue lobelias.

We ring the bell, and Grandmamma's widow's cap, with her wrinkled face below it, appears at the dining-room window. Before Grandpapa died that cap used to be a magnificent arrangement of lacey frills and purple ribbons. The gate jerks violently, and opens as if by magic. Our footsteps echo on the whitened stone pathway leading to the open front door, where Rose, Grandmamma's French house-tablemaid, welcomes us in her broken English, and ushers us into the dining-room. Red and blue Turkey carpet, round table with a plant in the middle, black marble mantelpiece, leather chairs, lace curtains, gay antimacassars—Grandmamma sits on a padded leather sofa. A child's chair of polished mahogany with a tall back is in my eyes the one desirable thing in the room, and I desire it with my whole heart. It is a darling little chair, and it seems silly that an old lady like Grandmamma should possess such a treasure.

Cousin Louisa, who lives with Grandmamma, but whose cousinship is distant and nebulous, is very kind, but her interest in us is apt to be of the improving kind. And with no mother to teach us I do not doubt that we needed a deal of improving.

Depression, and the sense of Sunday, thrown off during the hillside walk, settles down on us. I find consolation in Albert biscuits, which I am allowed to pick out from among the dry water kind all mixed together in the biscuit-barrel. My father sips his glass of sherry and chats easily to Grandmamma, and Harry and Cousin Louisa join in. Charlie gazes out of the window, though there is nothing to see except the houses in Dryden Place, an opening just opposite.

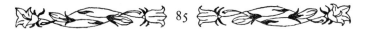

A gate clangs in Dryden Place. In the Sunday silence it sounds like doom.

"That's Miss Bateson's gate," says Grandmamma.

Miss Bateson, stout and elderly, comes out of her gate, and we all watch her going down the street, hearing the tap-tap of her leisurely footsteps on the pavement grow fainter till they die away round the corner into Blacket Lane.

We talk about Miss Bateson, and wonder where she can be going. We talk about Blacket Lane and how shady the trees are; we talk about Albert biscuits and water biscuits. Grandmamma has been to London to see Uncle Tom. She talks about the Park, and the grand carriages in the Row and the Princess of Wales, and oh! in one's weary heart one asks oneself, *isn't* it time to go?

It is, at long last.

"Good-bye," says Grandmamma, and kisses me.

"Good-bye, Honey," said Cousin Louisa, and takes my cheeks between her hands and kisses me on the mouth. It is a wet kiss, and I don't like it, but my sense of politeness makes me bear it with fortitude.

The gate clangs behind us, just like Miss Bateson's, and we face the long walk home through the streets. The straight endless row of shuttered shops seems to stretch on and on for miles and miles. Sober folk, the men in Sunday "blacks", are emerging from dull doors on their way to evening service. Solemn bells boom dolorously from gloomy churches. I am suddenly aware of intense fatigue and emptiness inside. A diet of biscuits, even Albert ones, is not sustaining. But I brighten up when a funeral comes along. Sunday was a good day for funerals of the humbler sort. The waving forest of black feathers which is the hearse, drawn by black horses with long manes and tails, comes slowly along the street. Sometimes a bunch of white feathers flutters gallantly among the black. Taught by Ann, an expert in funerals, I know what that means. The corpse must be a child, and I take a peculiar personal pride in the pomp and circumstance accorded to a contemporary. In the black-coated group following the hearse I mark down the chief mourners, noting particularly some poor little boy being led along, his eyes on the ground, abashed by this blaze of publicity, and with the cuffs of his little jacket adorned with white bands, called weepers. As the pathetic little procession comes abreast of us my father calls a halt, and he and my brothers stand bareheaded till it has passed. I feel we are part of the show.

Thus cheered on our way, we come at last to the North Bridge, where all the winds of Heaven meet, and I clutch my hat as I stand on tiptoe to look over the parapet and see the railway down below where it runs along under the shadow of the Calton Jail, and disappears into that terrifying black hole, the Calton Tunnel. A train is puffing its way towards the Tunnel. A Sunday train! Anything may happen to it, and I am glad I am not one of its Sabbath-breaking passengers.

And so at last we round the corner past the Theatre Royal into York Place. By this time Louis and I are faint with hunger. The mere thought of dinner spurs us on to a last effort, and we run up the front-door steps and almost tumble into the hall, clamorous for food.

Cold roast beef! beautiful cold roast beef!

"Hunger is the best sauce," says my father jovially, as he sharpens the carving-knife with a flourish and settles down

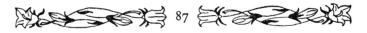

to carve succulent slices off the "Scotch side" of the sirloin. A proper sirloin this! A noble joint! of a juiciness and tenderness unequalled by any roast beef of Old England. Forbes pours claret and water—very little claret and a good deal of water—into our tumblers. The "eau rouge" of my youth.

Presently laughter, chased away by fatigue, returns to leaven the feast, so simple, yet so magnificent, and which is crowned by Christina's triumph, the apple tart *par excellence*.

Sunday draws to a close. Monday begins to cast its shadow. The lessons of tomorrow loom. Louis and I look at Schnorr's *Bible Pictures*. These begin with Adam and Eve and go on to Revelations. But we never get there. Cain and Abel, first as nice little boys with nothing on but a hat, and then grown-up and having a terrific set-to; Jacob, mean fellow, being blessed by a shaggy-haired bearded old Isaac in flowing draperies, with a distant view of the unlucky Esau striding home with a kid over his shoulder; the Flood, with all the wicked people drowning in enormous carefully curled billows, and angels in every corner of the sky emptying down buckets and buckets of water to add to the general mess, while the Ark, just like our toy one in the nursery, floats comfortably aloof from it all; David, a fine figure of youth, standing over a prostrate Goliath, out of whose forehead gushes a perfect torrent of blood, like a burst pipe in a thaw (which, long years after, my son Freddy painted a vivid red in a spirit of gruesome realism); these held our absorbed interest, especially if Aunt Louisa was there to point out the awful moral in every picture.

I look at these pictures now, and realise that they shaped

G

for me my ideas of Bible People, a race apart; not a bit like Me.

I don't remember any hymn-singing routine on Sunday evenings. But there was a time when Aunt Louisa plunged Louis and me into all the excitement of Moody and Sankey. She had become one of the fanatic followers of these emotional enthusiasts. The swing and vim of their hymns were attractive to children.

"Pull for the shore, sailor, pull for the shore," we sang. And through my mind would float confused visions of Leith Pier and a storm on the Firth of Forth; the picture of a curly-headed sailor boy in my bound volume of *Chatterbox*; and of Oban Bay, a fresh breeze whipping up little splashing waves, yachts dancing in the sunshine, and Me in a boat getting my first lessons in rowing from my father. No wonder that I thrilled to the tune and the words of that jolly rollicking hymn.

Less than two hours after dinner, about seven o'clock, a ceremonious tea meal was ceremoniously set out on the round table, with the best white-and-gold tea-cups, home-made strawberry jam in a glass dish with a slender stem, large round pats of butter in what Forbes called a butter-cooler, the loaf, and cake. Nobody wanted any, but it was part of Sunday. I remember sitting at the table wondering how anyone could ever want to eat bread and jam.

And so the memories of these early Sundays, when my father was alive, fade, blurred by the memories of later Sundays when he was there no more. They were changed. But then, when he died, everything for me was changed.

SCHOOLDAYS, 1876 to 1886

In old age one is apt to look back down the years with a certain wistfulness. That is how I might describe the feeling with which I pick up the book lying beside me, prettily bound in pink, ornamented with two gold birds and a gold bar across the middle.

On the bar is the title in black lettering,

THE HISTORY OF THE ROBINS
by Mrs. Trimmer.

Turning over the gilt-edged pages I still find charming the pictures of birds and branches, nests and children, as I found them when I was a child, but what most attracts my eye is the laurel-wreathed label pasted on the inside of the board, with this inscription:—

MADAME JULES KUNZ
Private Establishment for the
Education of Young Ladies.
Dux Prize for English, awarded to *Miss Hallard.*
19 Royal Circus, July 1878.

I was nine years old when, blushing and ecstatic, I received that prize from the hands of Monsieur Kunz himself. I had already been a "Young Lady" for more than two years, and was doubtless well away on the road to the education befitting the title.

Madame Kunz's School, the ways of it, the manners, the teaching, the friends—such things are clearer in my mind than the things of yesterday as is the first day when I first passed through the portals of 19 Royal Circus. My little brother Louis was with me. He was five years old. I was six and a half. Ann, our nurse, had led us by way of the Queen Street Gardens and Heriot Row down to the, to us, unknown regions of Royal Circus. It was May, and in the Circus Gardens, facing the crescent of tall grey houses, the trees were fresh with the green of spring, lilacs scented the air, and laburnums gleamed.

We mounted the wide stone steps, and were admitted through the dignified front door. Its polished handle was to be turned by me, morning after morning, through all my happy youthful years.

In the front hall we were met by, bent over, smiled at, and patted by, a little elderly lady in a black frilly dress and a cap all lace and ribbons over her grey hair. I learnt later to call her Miss de Dreux. She was Madame Kunz's sister. Into her care, after removing our hats and coats, Ann reluctantly delivered us, and was told to come back in two hours. Miss de Dreux then took a hand of each of us, and led us into the *grande salle*. Here, suddenly, innocent and unaware, we were plunged into a new world.

A world of girls. Rows of girls. Girls, big and little, seated at long desks on long leather-covered benches.

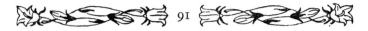

Girls, all summer frocks, pigtails and flowing locks, even grown-up hairpinned coils of hair.

And every eye of every girl turned to stare at us—us, two timid babes, blue-eyed, with long yellow curls, Louis in a belted tunic, me in a short frilled frock. Louis burst into tears. Attempts to comfort him were vain, so Miss de Dreux led him away to play with Jules, the youngest son of the house, in the back garden. I must have had more courage, for I allowed myself to be sat down at one of the long desks, next to Raoul, another son of the house. Miss de Dreux put a slate before me, and wrote a few figures on it, one below the other, with a line under them. She then put a slate-pencil in my hand, said something unintelligible and left me. I stared at the slate. I could make figures, but I had never seen a sum. I had no idea what to do with it. Raoul, an unusual looking little boy with fair hair cut *en brosse*, leaned over me smiling kindly. He pointed to the line under the figures, and whispered, "Six". I looked at him, and then wrote a large "6" under the line. Presently back came Miss de Dreux, said something else unintelligible, and wrote two letters under my sum. "T. B." (très bien). I seemed to have done what was required of me.

After that, I too, led by Raoul, went out into the back-garden, where, on the grass, and backed by three tall poplars, Louis stood, still weeping, while the kindly cook and the warm-hearted "Nana", and little Jules were all doing their utmost to comfort him. I put my arms round him, choking down my own sobs of sympathy. Then Ann came. Louis smiled again. The sun shone, and that was the end of the first day.

From Monday to Friday, for two weeks, the same routine.

Each morning, from ten to twelve, Louis wept. But I began to fit in. Dear "Little Miss Gray" (as, long years after, I loved to call her) gave me reading lessons out of a paper-covered book called *Step by Step*. I was apt and interested. She also set Louis beside her at her table and tried to teach him his letters. But Louis only bathed the alphabet with his tears. The end came. That fortnight over, we both got whooping cough, and I never saw a happier face than the face of Louis when Papa announced; "No more school this summer."

After that lugubrious start, with the autumn came new plans. I was to continue being a young lady at Madame Kunz's School, but Louis went to Mr. Hunter's School (Spoken of as "Hunter's") just across the street from our house, where there were little boys as well as girls. There he shed no more tears, but settled down cheerfully for the few years before going on to the Edinburgh Academy, like his brothers before him. As for me, my course was set—some twelve years of keen interests and lasting friendships lay before me. I was launched on my voyage of learning and loving.

I might speak of the next two or three years as being the era of "the little Schoolroom". In spite of its grander rivals, the *grande salle*, the *salle à manger* and the *salle d'études*, the "little schoolroom" stuck staunchly to its English title. Perhaps this was due to the English staunchness of "little Miss Gray", whose domain it was.

Here she ruled and taught. It was a sunny room, with a tall window looking out on the back garden with its three tall poplars standing up like sentinels, and four iron posts with ropes on which we watched the maids hang up the clothes on washing day. Opposite the window was a book-case, with numbered little compartments for our school-books. When one of these was allotted to me I swelled with pride and felt like a landowner. In the centre was Miss Gray's table, with its paraphernalia of mark-books, pens and pencils, and an inkstand. Behind that table, morning after morning, from nine till ten, sat Miss Gray, facing us, a restless row of ten or twelve little girls in short frocks and little aprons. Also the two youngest boys, Raoul and Jules, in blue suits and bow-ties. We sat on cane chairs with our feet perched up on the top bars, all agog, full of whisperings, apt to giggle and chatter, but keeping a wary eye on Miss Gray, who had us most admirably in thrall.

I like to remember her sitting there, a little woman, plain, plump, but with immense dignity of carriage. Her dark eyes, full of intelligence, looked one straight in the face— they could sparkle with anger, but more often with fun. We all liked her, and even the dullest of us made an effort to learn in response to her passionate desire to teach. She welcomed, as well as asked, questions. Upright and en- thusiastic, her soul was at the back of all she taught.

On the wall behind Miss Gray was a stand of rolled-up maps. For Geography lesson one of these was unrolled and hung up. We gazed with easy familiarity at the gaily coloured continents and countries. What a beautiful world of pinks and yellows, of blue seas and green islands!

Africa from a "lesson" point of view, was our favourite continent, being mostly sandy-coloured Sahara desert, with Timbuctoo in the middle, easy to point out with the long pointer when one's turn came. Egypt, too, had a certain interest because of Joseph, and the Plagues, and Pharaoh, and Moses among the bulrushes. We had learnt about them in our daily scripture lessons. We found Europe a very accommodating continent, with the easily recognized Italy "boot", and a pink Russia taking up most of the space, where we were only required to point out St. Petersburg and perhaps Moscow. Like the Grecian urn and beauty, that was all we knew or needed to know about Russia. When it came to nearer home, then prejudice and patriotism had their stubborn way with us. All very well for England to spread her patchwork quilt of counties before us. We viewed her with unsympathetic eyes. But unroll the map of Scotland, and here was Geography itself. What could a whole wilderness of maps display that could beat this land of ours? Look to the West, and there was pink Argyll, all broken up by long strips of blue sea, and lovely islands with romantic Highland names. Over the sea to Skye with Prince Charlie, and to Iona, where the long-ago saint built a shrine and raised a cross. Back to the East, and there was Edinburgh.

And here were we, actually in a house in a street in Edinburgh! Gleefully we pointed out the Firth of Forth, in which we had all bathed and paddled at one or other of the little villages on its coast. North Berwick, with the Bass Rock and Tantallon Castle, and over in Fife, Aberdour, its woods lovely in Maytime with the blue of wild hyacinths, and Largo, where Robinson Crusoe was born, Elie, with Macduff's cave and the rubies on Ruby Beach, and grey St. Andrews, with the links, the ruins, and the castle, and the echoes of the long-ago lullaby:

Hush thee, hush thee, do not fret thee,
The Black Douglas will not get thee.

We chattered, we pointed out, and compared notes on beaches and sand-castles and spades and shells, and jelly fish, and Miss Gray joined in and told us stories of Macduff, and Macbeth, and the Black Douglas. I had been to the Trossachs, and had seen Ben Lomond, "Ellen's Isle" and the "Silver Strand", so when the poetry lesson was from *The Lady of the Lake* the pictures in my mind flashed into unforgettable words. Lessons? These things were at the heart of us, and Miss Gray was there with us. That's the sort of person she was.

The same with History. History was for Miss Gray, and easily for us, a pageant of heroes and splendour, of pity and even tears, Scotland was of course our first love. Her history blazoned before our eyes the bravery of Wallace, Bruce and his indomitable spider, Bannockburn, Mary Queen of Scots and, best of all, Bonnie Prince Charlie, with tartans waving and banners flying. . . .

Little Arthur's England brought us good King Alfred and Harold after a page or two of blue-painted Britons with Druids and mistletoe—and so on to the lion-hearted Richard and his brave Crusaders, and the sad tale, with a pathetic picture, of the little princes in the Tower. And, of course, that hero of heroes for all little girls, the glorious and adorable Sir Walter Raleigh, cloak and all. We learnt the names of all the wives of Henry VIII, we loved Charles I and hated Cromwell, and after being a little bored by Queen Anne and the Georges, we ended up comfortably with our own Queen Victoria, and she, in our childish loyalties, was and would be ever the one and only heroine of the National Anthem.

Little Arthur's England—I have it still. I remember how I

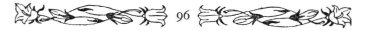

would open it and read the first words: "You know, my dear little Arthur" and then turn to the last page and read the last words: "I hope it will help you to understand bigger and better histories bye and bye." I don't know if it was "Little Arthur", but most certainly it was little Miss Gray who helped me to that understanding, awaking in me, sublimely unconscious, interest and energy for tackling these "bigger and better histories" in later years.

One of our lessons was to read aloud.

I do not know what children read in school these days, but the people who compiled our reading books must have been as deeply concerned about *what* we read as about how we read it—for our books were made up of extracts from great writers, interspersed with poetry from the great poets. I remember being charmed and amused by the *Sir Roger de Coverley* papers from the *Spectator*, while the translation of Pliny's letters to Tacitus describing the eruption of Vesuvius, and the lava pouring down on Pompeii and Herculaneum, must have made so deep an impression that it was still clear at the back of my mind when, many years later, I saw the smoke of Vesuvius above the Bay of Naples, and stood among the ruins of the cities.

Of all the valuable things we learnt in those early days in "the little Schoolroom" nothing, I think, was more valuable than the poetry, which we not only got by heart, but, tirred by Miss Gray's enthusiasms, also took to heart, laying the foundations of a love of poetry which has ever remained with me. Can I ever forget the stimulating joy of standing up and reciting:

> Cannon to right of them, Cannon to left of them,
> Volleyed and thundered.

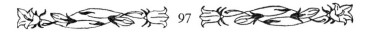

and all the time seeing in my mind's eye that brave Brigade, galloping, galloping into immortal glory? "Their's not to reason why!" Neither was it mine—the splendour and the tragedy were all in all.

And "The Schooner Hesperus!" with the ache in my heart for the skipper's little daughter lying on that forsaken beach,

> The salt sea frozen on her breast,
> The salt tears in her eye.

And the appeal of the incorruptible Casabianca, standing alone amid the flames, preferring death to disobedience! Oh, the pity of it! I felt it, Miss Gray felt it, we all felt it.

I think we regarded the "Queen of the May" rather in the light of a distinguished stranger, for no Queens of May ever reigned in Scotland, but we liked her, and sympathised with her eager desire to be up and doing—the lilt of her lines was easy to learn, and she lilted so many touching and interesting things that we could only rejoice when she, having "thought to pass away before" went on living and lilting for quite a page or two longer. Then for rollicking fun, could anything beat "John Gilpin and his Spouse", and that gay picnic at "The Bell" at Edmonton, and the screaming from the balcony when the wigless John went flashing by on his run-away steed?

And surely there was no resisting the charm of the dashing "Young Lochinvar" and his fair Ellen? "One touch to her hand, and one word in her ear" (and couldn't one just see the glint in his eye!) and in a trice they're off and away, all the wedding guests coming helter-skelter behind them! Then ho! for the "racing and chasing on

Cannobie Lee!" How we all laughed! How Miss Gray laughed! In gentler strain, could anything be sweeter than that dear little brook telling its own story and how it came "from haunts of coot and hern", chatter-chattering its way to "join the brimming river"? I knew quite a lot of chattering brooks myself. And I think that even we, young as we were, felt the strain of music linked with infinity in the haunting refrain:

> For men may come and men may go,
> But I go on for ever.

Many another poem could I speak of which sang itself into my heart and memory. But for me, best of all, the ever delightful blacksmith in his smithy "under a spreading chestnut tree".

Best for me, because I actually knew a blacksmith, just like Longfellow's, minus the chestnut tree, who lived on Tweedside in a jewel of a tiny village called Clovenfords, where I was taken every spring. My father and my brothers put up at the Inn, where Hogg the Ettrick Shepherd, and Sir Walter Scott, had put up before them—but Louis and I and Ann lived in the village blacksmith's cottage, with the smithy next door, and through the wall we could hear the bellows blowing and the horses stamping. My blacksmith, too, had "large and sinewy hands"—"swiney" as one of my own children misread it—and often did I stand and watch him shoeing a horse, and was allowed to put my small hands on the bellows and help blow the fire. So it is of my Clovenfords blacksmith, dark-eyed and black-bearded, in his smithy among the hills, that Longfellow brings back the memory.

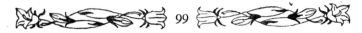

At ten o'clock Miss de Dreux rang the big brass bell in the hall. She did this every hour until two o'clock, when the day-girls went home. At the sound of the bell, doors would open and release girls talking and laughing; feet ran to and fro, as we all changed rooms for different classes. Each hour, silence changed to noise, and noise again to silence. A memory stays with me, of arriving late one morning to find all doors closed against me, like the gates of doom. The ticking of the grandfather clock in the corner seemed an echo of my anxiously beating heart. I could hear the voice of Mr. Robertson in the *salle à manger*, and perhaps the German tones of Madame Kunz in the *grande salle* with the Senior German class. Upstairs and down I heard the muffled sound of pianos, hesitating scales, or stumbling sonatas, and the guttural German voices of Miss Wehle and Miss Javrova the music teachers—all very awe-inspiring for an anxious culprit.

In the *grande salle*, from ten to eleven o'clock, Mr. Robertson taught writing and arithmetic. Seated at one of the long desks, I had my first thrill with real ink and a quill pen. Oh, the spluttering of that pen! And the messiness of the thin pink *papier buvard* that soaked up the blots! And the pages of alphabetical moral maxims we scratched and blotted in our copy-books!

For our sums we used slates, and slate-pencils, which would often give out a horrible screech as our small hands slipped on a line or figure, and this would be echoed by a screech of agony from everybody in the room. We did a great deal of rubbing out with the *torchon*, helped by a lick from a finger.

Mr. Robertson had a long red beard and whiskers

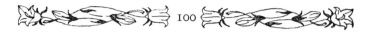

which tickled my neck as he bent over me correcting my sums. . . .

We had our first French lessons from Miss de Dreux. Hall's *First French Course*, all masculines and feminines, troublesome conjugations, and exercises to write at home. Before very long we were reading *Un Philosophe sous les Toits*—I cannot remember the author, but I know I had a sort of affection for that old philosopher and his meditations under his roofs.

It was dear Miss Bogen who gave us our first German lessons, only vocabulary, no books. She was a sweet, kind creature, and we all loved her. Later on, when Madame Kunz took us over, German became important, with Weisse's Grammar, Schiller, Goethe's "Faust" and Heine's poetry. But even in these early days we were growing daily more familiar with speech both in French and German.

Then, of course, there was music. There were two piano mistresses, both German, both very plain, both admirable teachers, though severe, both trained at Leipzig Conservatoire, which in those days was considered the last word for training "in all kinds of musick". Miss Javrova, who taught us little ones, had a very long nose. Though she was strict, she was kind and appreciative of effort. I was a nervously conscientious child, and took my practising seriously. "You must play this ten times over", Miss Javrova would say, pointing with relentless fingers to a jumble of crotchets and quavers. And, at home, on the old Broadwood piano in the dining-room, I would play and count, count and play, often with tears. But all the playing and counting brought their own reward, so I remember Miss Javrova with gratitude.

Miss Wehle, the senior music mistress, was so uncompromisingly plain as to be almost terrifying. Her eyes were black, cold and protruding, framed in long black curls like snakes. In spite of the snakes, perhaps because of them (there's no accounting for taste!), she got married, to a husband as plain as herself. They were married in Edinburgh, at the Sheriff Court, my father officiating, and I and my family were bidden to the wedding breakfast at 19 Royal Circus. It was quite a goodly company that sat round the long table in the *salle à manger.* I sat opposite the bride and bridegroom. He was in evening-dress. They sat as stiff as statues and looked as solemn as owls. The snakes, under some sort of bridal veil, held me spellbound. I never saw an uglier pair. Monsieur Kunz, rotund and charming, made a speech in German, French and English, which we all applauded loudly. The feast finished, the couple fled. And that, for me, was the unlamented end of Miss Wehle.

At half-past twelve there was a break. All the day-girls came crowding into the *grande salle,* where we relaxed at the long desks, laughing and chattering, while we ate our scones and "cookies" (one of each) handed round in baskets by Miss de Dreux and a maid called Jessamine. There was water to drink if we were thirsty.

The boarders had their lunch in comparative luxury, sitting at the table in the *salle à manger,* with Madame Kunz at the head, making tea in the tall brown tea-urn, while one of the boarders stood at the sideboard cutting slice after slice off a huge loaf. Little butter balls floated in glass butter-coolers, and there were home-made jams in pretty glass dishes.

When I was thirteen, my father died, and I think Madame

then felt me to be under her particular care. So I was brought into the *salle à manger*, and thenceforth had lunch with the boarders. I sat beside Edmée Kunz, then about eight or nine years old, and she and I would chatter happily together as we ate our bread and jam.

Strange to think that she and I, widely separated, still do our best, in long letters, to chatter happily together.

A close friendship grew up between my family and the Kunz family, to whose kindness and cultivated outlook, especially in foreign languages and music, I owe so much. My father, though born in Edinburgh, was of French parents, so with others of the same origin (and there were many in Edinburgh) friendship came easily. As children, we were used to having French cousins and friends as frequent guests in our house in York Place—Monsieur and Madame Kunz were Alsatians, he more French than German, she more German than French. They were tri-lingual, and also had an admirable knowledge of the English classics.

It is possible, therefore, that, knowing my background, Madame, at the very start of my being a pupil in the school, may have regarded me with a sort of proprietary interest.

A warm and grateful memory of that interest will ever remain with me. When my father lay dying, she came to see him. As she bent over him, her tears pouring down, I heard her say:

"Nellie will be mine!"

My father whispered his thanks, and I stood by, weeping.

When I was about nine years old, there came in a fashion to dress little girls like miniature Newhaven fishwives— striped cotton skirts, turned-up tunics of blue serge, striped cotton collars and cuffs and little aprons with pockets.

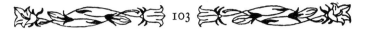

What to our elders was just a pretty style was for us a passion—*not* to be like a Newhaven fishwife was tragedy. Dear Ann soon succumbed to my urgent appeals, so I too came to school, radiant in serge and stripes. And then, one day, also in serge and stripes, came Frances.

It was one morning, after lessons had begun, that Miss de Dreux came in, leading by the hand a little girl. Such an enormously tall and broad little girl that we all stared aghast. Miss de Dreux introduced her to a smiling Miss Gray as a new pupil. The whisper went round: "She ought to be in Mr. Robertson's class!" Poor child! She stood facing us, her big hands thrust into the pockets of her fishwife apron. Her head, with its long pigtail of brown hair, was big, her face was big, and her big grey eyes gazed back at us, half fearful, half defiant. A chair was found for her, and she took her place at the end of the row, and lessons went on. Miss Gray asked her a few easy questions, while we became as one great eye and one great ear, watching and listening for her answers. Poor Frances, we found her shy and sensitive, and unaccustomed to teasing, flushing a deep red if any of us tried it on. But soon, quite soon, Frances and I joined hands, and she became my first real school-friend. Very shortly afterwards came her cousin, Edith, also very tall, but very fair, with a long pigtail like pale gold. And the three of us joined hands. So through all our school years, through all the long years to follow, going our different ways, making new friends, marrying, leading our own lives, always in spirit, and affection, our hands were joined.

At the mature age of eleven, I, with Frances and Edith, and the others, bade farewell to the little schoolroom and

H

moved into the *salle à manger*, where Mr. Robertson, already familiar to us with copy-books and the multiplication table in the *grande salle*, was in charge of the second English Class. With the change of scene and teachers came a change of atmosphere. With the Master came the Chaperone. In that capacity I chiefly remember Miss Bogen sitting at the window end of the long dining-room table, doing crochet work. We sat on a long bench up against the wall, facing the table and the Master's chair. There came in also a new ceremony. We were no longer plain "Frances", "Edith", but "Miss Frances", "Miss Edith", and so on. In a moment, in a trice, we were transformed. No longer "little girls", but "young ladies". And when, of a morning, after a good deal of jostling and noise we had taken our places, and Mr. Robertson entered the room, we all sprang to our feet as he bowed "good morning" to us and Miss Bogen.

It was in Mr. Robertson's class that we three, Frances, Edith and I, met, and took to our bosoms another friend, Connie, plain, plump and emotional. Her parents were in India. That alone put a halo round her head, gave her prestige. Every girl felt a special interest in her—so, I am sure, did Mr. Robertson. So did Miss Bogen. Once, the whole class listening in solemn silence, she recited "Little Jack Horner" in Hindustani.

Chota Jack Horna
Corna Mabeita.

The world for me was suddenly enlarged. I pictured rows of brown people and little brown children all sitting under palm trees reciting "Chota Jack Horna" for ever and ever.

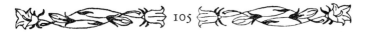

Mr. Robertson was a good and conscientious teacher. He had knowledge, and a certain modest enthusiasm that invited questions. We liked him, but with the uncanny intuition of children we quickly realised that he was no disciplinarian, and naturally we took advantage of that. Only at Monday morning's Scripture lesson, when Madame Kunz took Miss Bogen's place as Chaperone, did the poor man have some peace from our interruptions and chatter. A stern glance from Madame could quell the lightest whisper.

New ways, new books, new subjects, new steps on the stimulating journey to knowledge. Left behind us was "Little Arthur" with his pictures and clear-cut stories. History now loomed larger and graver than just hero-worshipping and villain-hating.

I remember a book bound in dark blue called *The History of Rome*. A splendid new venture this! We made friends with Romulus and Remus, and had deep sympathy for Romulus when Remus laughed and jumped over his wall. A whole pageant of Kings and Consuls, Spartans and Carthaginians, Hannibal, Brutus and Julius Caesar was spread before our eyes and impressed upon our young enthusiasms. The mythologies of Greece and Rome, Gods and Goddesses, heroes and nymphs, the stories of the Iliad and the Odyssey—these, in the shape of lessons became a procession of exciting adventures. I was, while still very young, familiar with the names of Jupiter, Mars, Venus and the rest, because my father loved to take us children out into the clear darkness of an autumn evening to point out the stars. And through his wonderful telescope, which seemed to bring the skies down to us, we gazed and wondered at Jupiter's moons, Saturn with his belt, and the red flashing of Mars. Evangelically-minded Aunt Louisa disapproved, and, in my hearing, sweepingly condemned the learning of heathen mythologies.

"Useless knowledge," she said sternly.

Next day, rather set up and perky, I announced this to my school-fellows. Miss de Dreux, standing by, overheard me, and cleverly did she take me up. "How", said she, "would you understand if I spoke to you of someone having "'Herculean strength'"?

For a moment I was baffled, then I saw the point and my mind took a leap forward. Words were not only sounds. There was reason behind them. And it was in Mr. Robertson's class that we began to tackle the derivations of words. Girls, in my day, did not learn Latin and Greek; but to sit down with a dictionary beside one, and a long list of words, not only to spell, but to find out how they came to be there at all, at least taught us that much of what we spoke and read had been gathered, like flowers from a garden, from the ancient tongues, and made into that gracious garland of sounds we call the English language.

Then I had to write my first essay.

"The subject and the title," said Mr. Robertson, "is to be 'My Summer holidays'."

I went home that day with dismay in my heart—I was almost in tears when I sat down and began:

"I spent my holidays in Callander"—and after that start my pen did not stop until I had covered two sheets of essay paper with the account of a picnic to Balquhidder. I have that essay still, and I still remember that picnic, the coach and three horses, the pass of Leny, Ben Ledi, Strathyre,

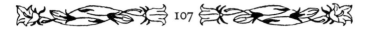

the river Teith, Loch Lubnaig and Rob Roy's grave.

> Ben Ledi saw the cross of fire,
> It glanced like lightning up Strathyre.

Can it be wondered that such lines conjured up for me visions of beauty and romance?

The years go by, I am in my teens, and pass on with my friends into the senior English class, with Mr. Maclaren for Master. And we become Monsieur Kunz's pupils for French. Old girls have left, new girls have come—but Frances and Edith and I are still together. Connie has gone, but Beatrice has taken her place, and stays, as my dear friend, for many happy years.

She was younger than me, clever, charming and musical. She left later to go to St. Leonard's School in St. Andrews, but not before I had got to know her in her delightful home near Granton, with the terraced garden stretching down to the sea.

Mr. Maclaren was a clear-thinking competent teacher. I suppose the ages of us, his pupils, ranged from about fourteen years to sixteen and even seventeen, and our brains from those of dear ever-smiling Mabel's at the bottom of the class to those of the keen ambitious few at the top. No easy task for any master.

Mr. Maclaren could not be called handsome, with what was called a "Newgate fringe" of greyish whiskers round his cheeks and chin, but there was that in his looks which commanded respect. He could be stern, and at times had need to be, but his command over us had nothing to do with the presence of Madame Kunz, who sat at some distance, seemingly absorbed in needlework. Indeed in

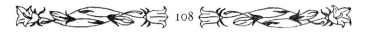

certain mischievous moods, when we tried our hand at some frivolity, we guessed that we had her amused sympathy, though she never voiced it.

As I grew, I hope in grace and certainly in understanding, I began to find in Mr. Maclaren an inspiring teacher. He had read widely, and was a judge of style. And as books made up much of my home background these qualities suited me well.

At the age of sixteen I and my friends were considered to be grown-up young ladies. We wore our hair done up in neat buns at the backs of our heads and our skirts reached down to our ankles. The last two years of school, happy, busy years, had been full of many and wide interests. Among them were Monsieur Kunz's French plays (which I have described elsewhere), written and produced by himself; music and the end-of-term concerts (terrifying ordeals!); piano lessons from Mr. Tom Craig, member of a well-known Edinburgh family of musicians, who taught me not only to play but to strive to interpret Beethoven. I had singing lessons with Blanche Kunz for teacher, which opened up for me vistas of joy and beauty in the songs of Schubert, Schumann and others, German and French and English. For me, too, Edinburgh's Child, there was always our incomparable heritage of Scottish song.

Strict school routine no longer applied to us elders. We attended lectures. Dr. Andrew Wilson, with his talks on anatomy taught us to wonder at and admire the way our bodies had been put together. In his lectures on the Bible, Dean Montgomery certainly turned our minds towards biblical understanding, and Monsieur Kunz's lectures on French literature spurred on Frances, Edith and me to

meet together in each other's houses for reading, with laughter and pleasure, the plays of Molière or Racine.

And so, at long last, came the day when, with an ache at my heart, I shut, for the last time, the wide front door of 19 Royal Circus. The "ten years of learning and loving" which had lain before me, now lay behind me. During those years, I think one aim had influenced all my teachers —I had been encouraged to raise my eyes to the hills of knowledge and wisdom, of truth and beauty. None can reach the summits, but to have them pointed out, to be taught to realise that they are there—that, in my humble opinion, should be at the heart of all education.

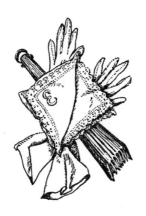

EDINBURGH DÉBUTANTE 1887

Late Autumn in 1887. The tang of the coming winter in the keen air. The "Season" is beginning. Princes Street's morning promenade has filled up once more after the long holidays. The shops have put away all the tourist displays of tartans, and the windows are decked out with the newest styles for the winter gaieties.

That winter was to mark an epoch in my life, the beginning of new and exciting experiences. I was to "come out" at the Hunt Ball. My brother Charles had arranged it all. He had the tickets, found me a chaperone, and pondered over my partners. He had also given his opinion about my frock (we called them "gowns" then), and ordered my bouquet.

Charles was already an experienced dancing man, at home in the Assembly Rooms, a W.S. apprentice, young, handsome, debonair, with many male friends and very popular with the ladies, young and old. Just the right sort of brother to launch a sister (with alas! no mother to smile approval) into Society.

III

Ever since I was sixteen, when I first put up my hair and let down my skirts, I had considered myself to be grown-up. But I had been still under tutelage, studying French and German and music, and many other subjects considered necessary and becoming for the intellectual and cultural development of the young ladies of those days.

I also went to parties and dances, given for what are now, I believe, called the "teen-agers". There I met my future partners in embryo, in the hobbledehoy stage of boyhood. We learnt manners together, they to bow and "request the pleasure of this dance", I to smile and accept with grace the proffer of an Eton-jacketed young arm.

And now I was eighteen, full-fledged, ready and eager to take wing. A Season of dancing and pleasure lay before me. The Hunt Ball was to be my first appearance in "Society" properly so-called. Everybody who was anybody already knew who were to be the débutantes of the year. Their chances of success and popularity were matters for discussion in drawing-rooms, and even in clubs.

Much depended on the dressmaker.

Two friends, Harriet and Edith, both older than myself, and wise with the wisdom of at least two seasons' experience in the fashionable world, led me, a humble catechumen, to a shop in the West End of Princes Street. Humbly following them into the hidden depths at the back and up a narrow staircase, we were ushered into a depressing little room, where, on a chair, beside a table littered with fashion papers, my feet on a pin-bespattered carpet, I awaited with beating heart my presentation to the presiding power, the French dressmaker.

She came, she saw, and I, to my secret joy, evidently

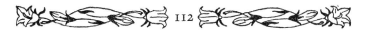

conquered, for as her appraising glance took in my trembling form, from my hat to the toes of my elegant boots, I felt her smile to be encouraging. I might be worth her skill. She could make a good job of me.

Then with what earnestness, with what absorbed concentration did Harriet and Edith and Mademoiselle discuss materials and styles. I was all ears, but my opinion was not invited.

"White, of course!"

"Ça va sans dire!"

"Silk, certainly."

"Mais oui!"

"Silver-bugled net for draperies?"

"Ah! Innocence! Charme!"

How low should be the neck? How infinitesimal or non-existent the sleeves? I, gently daring, pleaded for "not too low", and for even "the tiniest puff of a sleeve."

Harriet and Edith protested, Mademoiselle threw up her hands. Then she summoned her minions, and before my dazzled eyes they shook out billows of loveliness. Timidly I chose, and smiles approved my choice. Then I stood up. Mademoiselle measured me with her eye, and a minion measured me with a tape. My alas! hitherto comfortable waist-line caused murmurs of anxiety. But that could be set right. My corsets must be laced tighter. Comfort? Bah!

The ordeal was over. I was given to understand that if I trusted myself to Mademoiselle and her minions they would take me to their fashion-wise bosoms and turn me out the débutante *par excellence* of that season.

Nine o'clock in the evening on the day of days. There was excitement in the very air of the house.

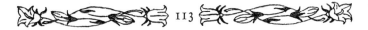

In my room, bright with fire and gas and candles, wardrobe doors gaped open, and scattered garments bestrewed the chairs. On my dressing-table lay my ivory-backed brush, a large pin-cushion, my lace-trimmed handkerchief, a green glass bottle with gold spots full of Eau de Cologne, and a sprinkling of hairpins. No rouge, neither powder nor lipstick—nature's own colours on cheek and lip were deemed ravishment enow for the "young ladies" of those days.

I held myself stiffly while Ann, my childhood's nurse, exultant over her nursling, laced up that nursling's first ball-dress. I held my breath to ease the ruthless process. That done, Ann fell back, clasping her hands in speechless admiration.

Before my mirror I stood a-gaze, seeing myself as others were to see me, and my heart rejoiced. My light brown hair, curly, and rippling, was in a simple coil at the back of my head; my neck and arms were bare and white and rounded, my waist trim and slim. My skirt, with its silver-bugled net draperies hung in silken folds to my feet, barely showing the tips of my white satin shoes.

Mademoiselle had surely made a good job of me.

Ann flung open the door to admit the cook and the table-maid, who had been waiting anxiously for a summons. Being Scots, they did not exclaim in extravagant rapture. But the expression on their faces was absorbed, even reverent.

"Yon's a bonny goon," said one.

"You suit it," said the other.

I was satisfied. Such praise was praise indeed.

Then Charles entered, my eager escort, shining in the glory of the occasion, with a pink carnation in his button-hole.

I buttoned up my long white gloves, took my large white fan in one hand and my bouquet of lily of the valley in the other, and stood among them, no longer the *ingénue*, but grown-up, a Society girl, conscious of my new dignity and my new charm of looks and style, waiting and wondering on the threshold of a new world of pleasure, bringing with it its own duties of manners and etiquette.

"Losh! There's the cab!" said the cook.

Wrapped in my evening-coat of an Indian Shawl pattern, and with what was called a "cloud" over my head, I set off with Charles on the great adventure.

And now must I close my eyes a moment, the better to conjure up the magic memories that throng my mind, a kaleidoscope of dreams.

I remember how in the dressing-room I met my chaperone Mrs. Brown, surrounded by a chattering bevy of girls, among whom her débutante daughter Beatrice was one of the prettiest. Merry voices bade me welcome, and presently, as other chaperones and their charges began to move towards the ballroom, Mrs. Brown gathered us, like chickens, under her matronly wing, and in modest silence we followed her, passing through the spacious ante-room, where crowds of delightful young men, several proudly conspicuous in hunting pink, others flaunting huge button-holes in their immaculate evening-coats and holding dance programmes in their white-gloved hands, watched us pass, keeping an eager look-out, ready to pounce on some favourite partner.

Slowly making our way among gossiping groups of young and old, the tinkle of laughter, bouquets held high scenting the air, silken rustlings as skirt meets skirt, we pass through the wide doors into the Assembly Rooms.

Can I ever forget that first breath-taking glimpse of brilliance and splendour which now opened before my unsophisticated but enraptured eyes? Far above one's head, from the ceiling, lofty and aloof, the crystal chandeliers hang delicately as if on threads of gossamer. From them, innumerable lights shine down, illuminating the length and breadth of that stately hall, where the floor stretches from shining distance to shining distance; lighting up the raised seats under the high-windowed walls, where the velvets and satins of bediamonded dowagers crush and crowd together; sparkling on jewelled bracelets as delicate wrists wave in graceful greeting.

In front, restless, excited, smiling, chattering, stand the girls, golden and brown heads turning and nodding, débutante white mingling with the rainbow colours of the already "out", ribbons on the bouquets fluttering, bouquets and girls one glowing garden of colour.

Among them stand I waiting, fidgeting with my pro-gramme. Partners swarm like bees round honey. The men I know find me quickly, and Charles, all aglow with pleasure and pride, the prince of brothers, introduces friend after friend. Bows, smiles.

"May I have the pleasure?" over and over.

"Yes!" and again "yes!" and again and again, triumph-antly, "Yes!"

Dambman's Band in the musicians' gallery strikes up the first waltz. Strauss is it? or Waldteufel? I don't know and I don't care. It is just for me music bewitching.

The room is divided into two by a tasselled cord, held by two attendants. Couples glide off into the wide spaces, swiftly turning, swaying with the new carefree lighthearted stepping which has replaced the languorous slip and slide.

My first claimant puts his arm round my waist, and in a moment life has become a dream of movement, music and ecstasy. An ecstasy that increases as the hours fly.

Waltz! waltz! lancers! not yet the kitchen kind, graceful and gay. A polka! whirl and spring, down the whole length of the room on one side, up the other hand-in-hand, hopping, skipping, laughing. "For a romping rollicking polka is the jolliest fun I know!" blares the band. A pause: then the reel. This is serious. The eightsome circles form, there is a bit of fussing about the right people for the right set. We wait, hands linked, arms at full stretch. A chord, then the full-throated yell which starts us off on a twenty-minutes madness. But a madness with method in it, for here are Highland names and Highland blood, so, no fooling! I note with awe the rapt expression on my partner's face. His eyes gaze into space as his leaps get higher—his frequent gasping shout seems an involuntary spasm of fierceness. A moment's breathing space, then on once more; the Strathspey, the Reel of Tulloch. Wilder the yells, our feet seem on springs. Then a long, last enthusiastic chord, and the band sinks back and mops its brow. Loud clappings come from the serried ranks on the raised seats. Breathless, reluctant, a trifle dishevelled, from delirious heights we drop again to the quiet levels of civilised behaviour. My partner bows, I curtsey, and my hand in his arm, we seek supper, mingling with a hot and happy like-minded crowd. Meanwhile the band, bless its gallant heart, starts off on the supper extras.

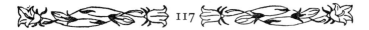

Champagne! Turkey! Pheasant! In a corner a Newhaven fishwife in her striped skirts is opening oysters without pause; exotic luxuries, pine-apple, peaches, are piled high—Ah me! The plentiful days! Waiters fly round, anxious, deferential, where we sit at the flower-decked tables. Bouquets a little dashed perhaps, hair needing the extra hairpin, my silver-bugled net missing a bugle or two, but *qu' importe*? Eyes sparkle, voice echoes voice, laughter rings again, the popping of corks, and in quiet corners, demure flirtations behind waving fans.

On with the dance! Hours seem minutes. Outside, in the sleeping city, unheard, unheeded, the church clocks have struck three. Some chaperones, a little anxious about late hours, begin to collect their reluctant charges. Mine is more lenient. I have still time for the last thrill, surely the apotheosis of a Hunt Ball. "D'ye Ken John Peel?" Irresistible! My partner seizes me, we are past bowing!

Oh, the reckless fun of it! The pace, the swing, the sound of the horn! Surely this will go on for ever!

But—the end comes, with laughter and cheering.

The end. But for me a glorious beginning!

"Good-night! Good-night!"

"Are you going to the New Club Ball? May I have the first dance?"

"Good-night! Good-night!"

"Are you all ready girls?" from Mrs. Brown.

Charles pleased, even *exalté*, hands me into a cab, and as he sits beside me, and we jolt and rattle over the stone setts homewards, he is kind and appreciative, praising my looks, my behaviour, and my success.

Home. Ann is awake and alert, ready to unlace me and to

brush my hair, and eager to hear all about it. She pulls the flowers in my bouquet off their wires and puts them in water. I watch her, my head still in a whirl, as I sit before the fire slowly drinking hot milk. And so to bed. To sleep? Yes. Perchance to dream? Maybe!

CHIEFLY AUNT LOUISA

In my old age, memories of my early years come thronging thick and fast, fleeting phantasmagoria, part of the sub-conscious background of childhood. Among them I see hover the pale shades of two old ladies. One is tall and thin, with a long aristocratic face and slender trembling hands. She was my mother's aunt. We called her Aunt Barbara. I knew that she was considered to be "not quite right" in her mind. Ann, our nurse, spoke of her quite simply as "puir auld body". I seem to see her as for ever weeping, even when she smiled, and I can still feel how her kisses, wet with perennial tears, damped my childish cheek, and I had to wipe them off surreptitiously for fear of giving offence. My brother Louis and I associated Aunt Barbara, and wet kisses, with St. Andrews, where she lived, and where Ann used sometimes to take us to see her—a joyful journey, first by steamer to Burntisland, and then in the leisurely train along a coast made up of little towns, green links, and yellow beaches.

I

The vision of a tall figure in black, with lace cap and collar, a long gold chain, and many brooches, with smiling face and streaming eyes waving to us from the window of a dull little house in a gloomy little street, is all part of a picture, deep in the dawn of memory, made up of grey archways, waves breaking along shining sands, and in the end, a grass plot in that lovely burial-ground in the shadow of the ruins of a grey Cathedral—And after that, no more wet kisses, no more dull little house, no more St. Andrews, no more Aunt Barbara. Louis and I knew that she was dead.

The other shade was great Aunt Fanny. She seems to fill a dim but warm corner of my heart. She was "Grand-mamma's" sister, and lived with her in Blacket Place. When we were taken there on duty visits it was Aunt Fanny who lit up for us many a weary hour spent in that formal dining-room by playing spillikins with us. Sometimes she sang to us in a soft little voice, with me on her knee, while the grown-ups talked to "Grandmamma".

Dear Aunt Fanny. She was little and sweet, and rather dumpy, with a face muffled round with lace and ribbons, a face which radiated goodness, where the smiles were all wrinkles and the wrinkles all smiles. She lived and moved in a kingdom of kindness. And even as I describe her, lo! she is gone, and Louis and I, racing along the sunny paths of the Grange Cemetery, shout out, "Here's Aunt Fanny's grave!"

And so these pale shades of aunthood vanish, and Aunt Louisa reigns alone. She has been there all the time, a constant presence—pervading and intimate.

I turn as I write to look at the painted head of a little girl in my picture of the French family group, a baby of three, rosy-cheeked, looking out at the world with bright

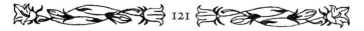

intelligent eyes, an earnest of the vivacious personality which became for us "Aunt Louisa", the "Auntie" of my childhood, remaining our affectionate, vaguely irresponsible aunt all through the years of a long life, kind-hearted and gay, with a gaiety hampered at times and harassed by a sombre religiosity.

Children seem to find little difficulty in reconciling contradictions in the conduct and precepts of their elders. Aunt Louisa denounced Drama as wicked. My father loved a good play, and we children were early initiated in the joys of the theatre. In my eyes my father could never be wrong, yet there was a half-conscious reservation at the back of my mind that Aunt Louisa was, religiously considered, probably in the right. But even then I dimly realised that in the banning of what she called "worldly pleasures", Auntie was really struggling against a natural bent. Mercifully for all concerned her sense of humour, and the irrepressible *joi de vivre* inherent in her French blood, would come bubbling up, banishing for the nonce the grim shadows of her fierce Protestantism.

I never learnt how or when she became so violently anti-Catholic. Her father, my French grandfather, was a Catholic, and she regarded him with adoration. As we grew older we used to wonder how she fitted him into the barren scheme of salvation which so possessed her. Once my brother Harry asked her about this. She hesitated, loving admiration at war with stern creed. Then love lifted her into his own heights, above all prejudice. Her actual words have not stayed with me, but this I understood. She believed that for one so dear and good as her father our Father in Heaven would assuredly keep one of his many mansions.

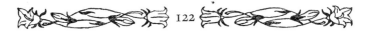

We children took Auntie and many other inconsistencies for granted. We were Episcopalians and went to St. Paul's Church in York Place, but in our country holidays my father would take us to the Parish Church, or even to the Free Church. Many of our intimate friends were of those persuasions and were all warmly welcome in our house. But so also was Father Rigg, who lived in the Priests' House beside the pro-Cathedral, and who enjoyed many a good glass of wine in my father's company. Aunt Louisa and Father Rigg were good enough friends, but many and many were the religious arguments between them which rolled about my childish ears like thunder among hills. The Padre was good-tempered and humorous, but Auntie, striving with all her might to refute the arguments of an astute mind, would get scarlet in the face and fling out texts at him like poisoned darts, which glanced off his priestly armour like so many harmless reeds.

There were occasional clashes of opinion between Ann and Auntie about religious experiences for the very young. I remember the first visit to Edinburgh of that extraordinary couple of American evangelists, Moody and Sankey. Aunt Louisa was caught up and swept off her feet by a wave of religious fervour. She went to all the meetings, for a whole week she lived and moved in an atmosphere of emotional piety. Sankey invented a new style in hymns, with tunes that were either sentimental or rollicking. Auntie used to play them, with Louis and me standing beside her carolling like birds, so that the echoes rang with "Hold the Fort" and "Jew-els, precious Jew-els!" Ann did not object to the hymns, but she maintained a distinctly aloof attitude to mass revival meetings for children, and she disapproved of

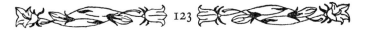

Moody's passionate appeals regarding the soul. The Scot looks on the soul as his own private concern. The less said about it the better. However, we took no hurt, and when the American pair went away the excitement went too. Nothing was left but the hymns.

Auntie was the kindest and most indulgent of aunts, and Louis and I loved her dearly. Louis was her particular pet, but as he was mine too I felt that to be quite as it should be. He was an adorable little boy with his golden curls and endearing lisp.

Auntie lived in rooms (which she always spoke of as "my lodgings") in North-West Circus Place. Sometimes Louis and I would spend a Sunday afternoon there, a rare pleasure. The lunch itself was a treat, though the only thing about it that stays in my memory is the particularly superb rice-pudding. Rice-pudding at home was a dreary duty, rice-pudding at Aunt Louisa's was a feast.

And after lunch Auntie would take us to the Children's Service at the church of her evangelical choice, St. Vincent's. It was so small that it gave me a delicious feeling of playing at church and I much preferred it to the wider spaces of our own St. Paul's in York Place. In St. Vincent's the seats were high and the hymns were hearty,

"Singing, Glory! Glory!! Glory!!!"

Louis and I perched on hassocks the better to let ourselves go, let go with such devout enthusiasm that Auntie regarded us with pride, and presented us in the porch to all her friends —and after these thrills, and not a little puffed up with our religious success, we would go back to Auntie's big sitting-room, and sit on the rug before the fire while she read to us out of the *Sunday at Home*, or told us stories about her friends, who were most of them unimaginably good, and either died early or, like one called Hannah, would lie for years on couches of pain repeating hymns. And one called Ellen White, who lived in Jersey, not only said hymns but wrote them.

"Home, Home, I would go Home!" said Auntie, quoting Ellen White and looking sentimental. But she could never remember the next line, which was tantalising.

In my very early years I think Auntie's stories of angelic examples and sometimes of awful warnings inspired me with a passionate desire to be "good". She filled the nursery bookshelves with books which she bought at the Tract Society's Shop on the Mound. My first instincts regarding charity to the poor and the horror of slums must have been derived from such moving romances as *Froggy's Little Brother*, and *Jessica's First Prayer*; while the "Golden Ladder" series preached to me an inspiring gospel of youthful good deeds.

Auntie loved tracts, and bought quantities of them at the same shop to distribute among her friends and acquaintances. She felt it to be her mission to spread what she conceived to be religious truth. Louis and I were much attracted by the neat bundles of brightly-coloured little books and pamphlets. But once we got into sad trouble with Ann because of these tracts.

It was at Leven, in Fife, on a fine Sunday morning. Ann must have been out of the way when Aunt Louisa was seized with the idea of turning Louis and me into little missionaries. We probably looked the part with our innocent golden curls and in our Sunday clothes. Auntie escaped with us to the churchyard near by, where the congregation were coming out of church and moving in sober groups down the

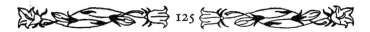

path. She filled our hands with tracts in the gayest colours and with the most appealing titles, and bade us hand them to those godly passers-by. We were filled with pride. I know I felt like the good children in Auntie's books.

A lady, beautifully attired in a lilac dress and bonnet came by. I picked out a tract and offered it to her. She gave me a gracious "thank you" and a charming smile. This was indeed to taste the sweets of missionary enterprise. This was glory.

And then came Ann! Ann, her usually mild countenance thunderous with disapproval. Unmindful of Aunt Louisa's indignant protests and our tears of disappointment, she dragged us ignominiously away from the scene of our short-lived public triumphs back to the prim paths of nursery-dom.

I must have been a very small girl when the magic of the word "France" began to penetrate my consciousness. Aunt Louisa spoke of "La Belle France", and I think I began early to have a sense that to be partly French was a superior thing to be.

A little nursery scene which comes to my mind seems to me to prove that.

I would be about four years old I suppose, and the echoes of the Franco-German war were still ringing in the grown-up people's talk which reached my childish ears. I remember being shown a letter which had come by balloon post from cousin Bernay during the siege of Paris. I heard that he and the people in Paris had had nothing to eat but dogs. I gathered that this was horrible, but very brave.

One day, Auntie, the deft-fingered, came into the nursery with two beautiful paper cocked hats she had made, one blue and the other green, in her hands. Louis and I gazed at them with joy, and Auntie told me to choose which I should like. All children I think prefer blue to green. I wanted the blue hat, but I saw the longing look in the eyes of Louis. I chose the green. The hats were put on and Auntie gazed adoringly at the effect of the blue on Louis' long fair curls.

"You are a real little Prussian!" she cried. Then, turning to me, she said consolingly, "but green is the *French* colour!" How my heart lifted! My colour sacrifice had not been in vain. To be French, that was reward enough.

French names, French cousins, the sound of spoken French in my ears, these things are woven into my earliest memories, as are also the stories Auntie would tell us of her childhood's days in France. Although she was born in Edinburgh, all her fondest reminiscences centred round places in Normandy. Many were the vivid and entrancing pictures her words painted for us. I can almost see that garden in—Avranches, was it?—that lovely garden with the wonderful swing, where charming young military officers came a-visiting, who used to play with the little daughter of the house.

"Such a high, high swing!" said Auntie, with eyes turned heavenwards as if gazing into illimitable space.

"They used to swing me high up into the air, but I was never afraid."

And there flashed before my inward eye the vision of a swing reaching heights which no swing had ever reached before, with a small but intrepid Aunt Louisa clinging to the ropes and screaming with joy, while gallant young men in gay uniforms vied with each other to swing her ever higher and higher.

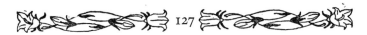

"My father was so afraid I should fall," said Auntie, "that he had another swing made for me, lower and safer, which at every upward swing plunged me into a lilac tree. I can smell that lilac now!" And Auntie gave a long sniff of dreamy delight.

Then she would tell us of the Convent School, it may have been in Avranches, where she went when she was eight years old. She had in these later years become so violently protestant that it was almost in apologetic tones that she spoke of the kind nuns in that school.

"They were very kind to me," she said, with a tender light of reminiscence in her eye. "La petite Anglaise" they called me. We used to have a slice of bread and butter for lunch, but as I was a favourite I had a pear as well. Such a big, juicy pear!"

Such succulent appreciation was in Auntie's face and voice that my mouth watered in sympathy.

"Once," she went on, "I did a dreadful thing. I dropped my piece of bread and butter on the floor."

She paused and looked at Louis and me, listening absorbed, to this long-ago drama.

"And," said Auntie, "I was punished. Can you guess how?"

Now Auntie used to read to us such lurid tales out of the *Christian Herald* about the doings in nunneries that we waited breathlessly to hear of some awful and painful penance.

"They made me eat that slice of bread and butter with the butter side turned *down*," said Auntie solemnly. Then she laughed; we all laughed. It was an anticlimax certainly, but a relief to know that even nuns had their human side!

Avranches! The name of that little Norman provincial

town, which I have never seen, rings like a bell through all my fast-dimming memories of long ago. As a child for me it was a place familiar, altogether charming, where lived gay and delightful people, the *dramatis personae* of Aunt Louisa's tales, even when she was grown-up and paid long visits to the haunts of her childhood. I could not know, nor did she herself seem to realise, that in those tales of hers, so full of colour and laughter, there yet sounded the knell of the France she loved, the passing of an *ancien régime*, of a place where an impoverished aristocracy, living in a modest but elegant retirement, still clung to a dying code of good manners.

Louis and I came to regard many of these people like old friends, albeit with a touch of fairyland glamour about them.

We grew quite fond of M. de Montallet, the courtly old gentleman with no teeth and a lisp.

"He was so very polite," said Auntie, "that sometimes it was quite embarrassing. Once when he had come to call I had a fit of sneezing. I sneezed and sneezed, and at every sneeze M. de Montallet rose and made me a low bow and solemnly lisped:

'Mademoithelle, je vous thalue!'

"At which," said Auntie, "I could hardly sneeze for laughing or laugh for sneezing."

Then there was old Baron de Pirch. He gave a party once, and Auntie and a group of English ladies arrived early and were shown into the salon. In the corner of the salon there was a curious little tent affair with curtains. To the amazement of the visitors the curtains suddenly parted and a powdered old head popped out.

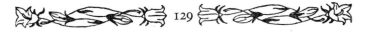

"Excuse me, ladees," said the head, "I am at my toilette!" and in popped the head again.

For ever cropping up in the stories, delightful, debonair, was the curé de Ketreville, a squire of dames, and an arbiter in religious controversies. A heated argument had arisen between fiercely Protestant Aunt Louisa and an equally staunch Catholic lady.

"Dites donc, M. le Curé" (and here Auntie's voice always took on a note of pretended guilelessness), "est-ce que Saint-Pierre etait marié, ou non?"

Then did M. le curé, in the person of Auntie, draw himself up and purse out his lips.

"*Certes*, Mademoiselle," said the curé, "il était marié!"

"O-Oh! M. le curé!" collapse, in Auntie's tones, of the Catholic lady, and her own triumph.

I remember, and the memory still brings a smile, how the Populace, the gay and excitable French Populace, figured so largely in Auntie's stories. A Populace ever ready to hold up its hands in horror, or give vent to voluble vociferations.

It did both when Auntie on horseback fell, horse and all, into the quicksand near Mont Saint-Michel, and had to be hauled out with ropes.

"Ces Anglais cherchent la Mort!" it proclaimed to Heaven (Auntie doubling the parts of victim and crowd).

And when, in a Paris pension, the wardrobe fell on Auntie with a crash, and the pension Populace rushed to the spot in time to see an unhurt and smiling Auntie emerge from underneath, it cried out with one accord:

"C'est un Miracle!"

When we were children Auntie would sometimes go for trips abroad, accompanying Grandmamma and Grandpapa, and a friend of her own, a diminutive little poppet of a woman, with a strong Northumbrian burr, whom we knew as "little Miss Grant". Louis and I would be taken by Ann to the Waverley Station to see them start. The ladies wore black bonnets with flowers in them. The travelling-trunks were huge and tied up with ropes. In the carriage there were waterproofs and umbrellas, and Auntie had an alpenstock for the Swiss mountains. It was felt to be a solemn occasion, and we all hoped they would come back safely.

Auntie used to tell of the adventure which befell "little Miss Grant", who lost her ticket, and ran up and down the Paris platform wringing her hands and crying:

"J'ai *perghdu* mon billet! J'ai *perghdu* mon billet!", till a kind French guard caught her, and put his arm round her, patting her shoulder and saying consolingly,

"Calmez-vous ma petite dame! Nous trouverons le petit billet!"

Switzerland now became Auntie's Eden, her land of promise, the place of delights. Into her stories came the amusements of travelling by "diligence", enthusiastic descriptions of snow summits, glaciers, pine forests, tales of her prowess on some of the lesser heights, the Saint-Bernard, the Monks, the Dogs, the food, the guests; we almost saw them all with our own eyes. I longed to behold the majesty of Mont Blanc, the beauty of Chamounix, the blue of the Lake of Geneva, a blue with which no blue of sea or sky could ever compare.

I have by me a letter from Geneva, in Auntie's beautiful printing, so that I might read it without grown-up help—the date is June 14th, 1876. In it she tells, in her own delightful way, of the sail on the Lake, a lovely walk, a wonderful

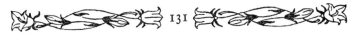

drive, and of the flowers. "More flowers than grass! Such
beauties! Pink! Blue! Yellow! Purple!" And all interspersed
among the clear lettering are pen-and-ink sketches of the
flowers, and one of "a nice fat lady" staying in the pension,
and even one of the "big ice puddings" they had on Sundays.

There were messages for "Papa", and for "my wee
Coozles" (her pet name for Louis), and it ends with "lots
of Kisses" from my "affectionate Auntie".

Ann must have put it away for me to keep, and among so
much that is old and treasured I have kept it all these long
years.

Through all Auntie's stories, told with such verve and
vividness, there ran, like a many-coloured thread, her own
personality, dowered with many little elegant gifts and
graces. She was no mean pianist, adventurous and skilful,
revelling in virtuosic variations of operatic airs, but ever
ready to come down from these impassioned heights to play
duets with me, filling out the weak treble of my small hands
with a gaily enthusiastic bass, so that "Home to our
Mountains" and "Beautiful Star" had for me all the later
thrill and sonorousness of Bach and Beethoven rolled into
one.

Then she drew, and she painted in oils, copying the old
masters with extraordinary neatness and skill. Such artistic
activities were looked upon as polite accomplishments in
Aunt Louisa's young days. But even to these she would
bring some little vagrant touch of originality, so that one
might say that she made an Aunt Louisa picture out of a
Murillo!

She took a stimulating interest in our nursery daubings.
Though I remember there was a horrid little girl called

Dolly whom she used to hold up as an example to us. Louis and I were given to painting the pictures in *Chatterbox*, laying on the colours with a fine, free, careless rapture, but with a lordly disregard for outline. Now Dolly never did that. Dolly gave every leaf of every tree its exact quota of green. Dolly was careful that the rosy cheeks of the picture children did not run amuck among their yellow locks. I was madly jealous of Dolly; and yet, when Auntie once praised one of my artistic efforts by saying "that is nearly as good as Dolly's", I nearly burst with pride.

But it was in the fashioning of paper flowers that Auntie's Frenchly artistic soul found its real outlet. It was perhaps her outstanding accomplishment. Those were the days when people believed in holding the mirror up to nature, and you could pay Auntie no greater compliment than to mistake her marvellous imitations for real flowers. And in the manipulation of an infinite variety of little brushes and implements, the dyes, the little tricks in the curling of leaves and petals, the blush on the roses, the velvet sheen on the pansies, and in the infinite pains she took to make her paper blossoms look beautiful as well as natural, I maintain that she triumphed over foregone conclusions, making an art out of an artifice. The little posies of mixed blooms were treasured possessions of many friends, and were kept under glass-cases like French clocks. But she delighted too in their use as table decorations, and there was a strange elegance in the arrangement of her scarlet geraniums in specimen glasses mixed with real maidenhair fern, as one saw them set among the sparkle of glass and silver on the long damask-covered table of ceremony.

But Auntie had also a gay little spirit of mischief which

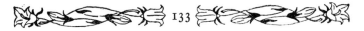

delighted in taking people in, and she loved to see some keen flower-lover plunge an unwitting nose into one of her luscious-seeming roses, and draw back with cries of amazement, or perhaps with a hand over a pricked nostril.

Poor Auntie! When, after my father's death, it was thought fitting that she should leave her pleasant rooms, her beloved "lodgings", and come and live with us in our house in York Place, I am sure it was a sacrifice made for our sakes. For it cannot have been altogether easy for her. As we and she grew older, we went our different ways, and our ways were not always hers. When I "came out", and paying calls was the fashion, my brother Charles, strict regarding the proprieties, insisted on our having an "at home" day, and told Auntie she must act as chaperone and receive callers. So, very much under protest, every Friday afternoon Auntie would dress herself in her best silk gown and smartest cap, and sit in her armchair by the fire in the drawing-room, prepared to receive visitors. Poor dear, she hardly knew any of our young friends, but they were all very respectful to her, and sometimes some particularly nice young man would pay her pretty compliments, and she would bridle and smile and pout and shrug her shoulders, and enjoy a little renaissance of her younger, sprightlier years. As a young woman she must have been very pretty, and she was still slender and upright, with small hands and extremely pretty feet, of which she was justifiably proud.

I gathered, from little things she said, that there had once been a lover, far back in the days when she and her father kept house together in Scotland Street, entertaining there many a distinguished guest, even members of the banished French royal family. The lover was an army officer and was killed in a Chartist riot. That much she let me know, and I could only suppose that that was the reason she never married. A large print of Canterbury Cathedral hung always in her room. She kept it, she said, in memory of him. But whether he had lived in Canterbury or was buried there, or for what reason it was so precious, I never knew.

And so the years passed and I married, and my brothers went to live in a flat in Great King Street, and in course of time left Edinburgh. So Auntie came to live with me in George Square and was called Auntie by the new generation. She led what one might call a rather remote life, divorced from community cares, occasionally taking out her paper-flower materials, but never completing a flower; sometimes sitting at the piano and playing over the old airs she knew; gradually, in her real, always graceful old age, withdrawing more into herself and her old memories, telling her old stories over and over again, confusing them very often. Her memory began to fail, and one day I found her gazing out of the window at a house on the opposite side of the Square.

"That," she said, "is the house where I was born."

"Oh no, Auntie," said I.

She turned on me.

"Were you there?" she asked sternly.

"No, Auntie, of course not."

"Well," said Auntie, "I *was*."

She went on dreamily, "I remember it *quite, quite* well. My father was at the war, and my mother was abroad at the time." I left it at that.

She was very proud of her Christian names, and when I was a little girl I disliked my own names and envied Auntie hers.

"Louisa, Frances, Margaret," she would say, with an impressive pause between each. And then, "beautiful names", she would add complacently. With my whole childish heart I agreed with her.

She was tended faithfully and devotedly by her maid, Barbara, who took the kindest pains in making her look sweet and nice. And she did look very nice and very sweet, even on her death-bed. She died of no special illness in July 1903, at the age of eighty-seven. During the last days of her life she wandered in her speech, going back to the French language she loved, murmuring lines of poetry or the hymns of her long-ago childhood:

"Home! Home! I would go Home!"

Dear, affectionate, amusing Aunt Louisa! Did you perhaps, at long last, remember the next line?

K

MY EDINBURGH DOCTORS

I love and remember Edinburgh for many things, for her beauty, her dignity, her much learning. But chiefly does my heart turn to her when I call to mind all those things, even the places and the names, that belong to her medical life and fame. These for me had, and in many a tender memory still have, a beauty peculiarly her own, a beauty of the spirit, speaking of lives set apart, devoted, ennobling. For me there was beauty even in the medical buildings and colleges, where the teaching of a humane science was as the preaching of a dedication. Beautiful, too, the great Infirmary and the hospitals, within whose walls the untiring thought and labour of an elect company was spent in service to the sick, and in showing to the young student with what gentle respect that high service should be approached.

Many a time and oft have I passed on a late afternoon through the grey stateliness of Charlotte Square and the West End streets and marked, with a stirring of the heart, how the quiet carriages stood before so many doors, waiting

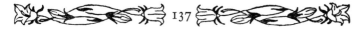

for the helpers and healers to set forth anew upon their Father's business. For it was the doctors, and the teachers in laboratory and classroom, the workers in research and experiment who were, and must ever be, behind all that I so love to look back on. So, my thoughts turning gratefully to the doctors I knew, and to those especially who, through the long years of my life in Edinburgh, ministered to me and mine, I am impelled to write down what I remember about them. I am well aware that no tribute of mine can add anything to their secure prestige. Many of them have long since passed to a well-won peace; but it may be that from where they are they will look down and forgive my humble and belated acknowledgment of what I owe them.

My record begins in early childhood. I see myself, a little girl, playing with my brother Louis in the nursery of our home in Edinburgh and being called by Ann, our nurse, to come at once and be tidied, for Dr. Malcolm was waiting downstairs. Dr. Malcolm was our family physician. Ann used to tell us that he had brought us all (and there had been nine of us) one by one in his black bag to my mother. But by the time my memory of him begins to take shape there was no Mother, and a sister and two little brothers were for me just names on a white cross in the Grange Cemetery. But I knew that Dr. Malcolm was responsible for my being there at all, and that Louis was his last, and alas! fatal gesture of generosity to my mother, for she died a few days after his birth and I was only sixteen months old. Aunt Louisa used to tell Louis that when he was a new baby he was bright yellow all over, and that Dr. Malcolm only kept him alive by feeding him on gin. Louis was always rather proud of his dissipated start in life, but I was glad that Dr. Malcolm was kind enough to save my little brother for me, even in this unusual manner.

I have no very clear memory of Dr. Malcolm at my bed-side, but I remember well those periodical visits of his, when Ann would take Louis and me down to the dining-room where he was waiting for us, a tall dignified man with reddish whiskers, dressed in a long blue "surtout" coat with a velvet collar. His keen blue eyes were fixed on us as we entered and politely shook hands, and as bidden, and still politely, put out our tongues. Routine practice this; but once Ann said to me, "Show the doctor your loose tooth."

Innocently I pointed to it—and the next moment I was in tears. But when he placed his stolen goods in my small palm I forgave him. All the same, Louis and I bore him a secret grudge, being convinced that he was the author and instigator of the not infrequent doses of vile medicines administered to us by Ann.

So, when once in some nursery book we came across a rhymed couplet having for second line "Slam the door in the Doctor's nose!" not even Keats' Watcher of the Skies with his new planet could have felt more elated. We bided our time.

I can only imagine what must have been the startled amazement of our benevolent physician when, on his next visit, his two usually well-mannered little patients rushed into the room, and instead of putting out their tongues, danced round him shouting at the tops of their voices,

"Slam the door in the Doctor's nose! Slam the door in the Doctor's nose!" The rest—of that story—is Silence!

One last brief glimpse of Dr. Malcolm, when he, my father and Ann, with Louis and me, stood round the bed of

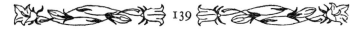

my brother Charlie, looking at his face, brilliantly scarlet, and hearing the doctor say "Scarlatina. Not Scarlet Fever." So nobody worried, and when I got a scarlet face shortly after, nobody worried. And it may be thanks to Dr. Malcolm that I am alive to tell the tale!

And here Dr. Malcolm vanishes from the picture. I never heard why, or what became of him. And with him, and others of his type, vanished, I think, something that had value. He lived in stirring times for the medical profession, when a new and wondrous world of discovery and knowledge was opening out, and the younger men were stretching eager hands to grasp it. Perhaps Dr. Malcolm was too old, too set in his ways to take advantage of it. But was there not something to be said for judgment born of long acquaintance with the family and their health idiosyncrasies? In an age, when there were no mechanical aids to diagnosis (I don't remember even having a thermometer thrust into my mouth), doctors had perforce to trust to their own intuition and powers of observation. Well, after all, so did, and so still do, the ancient weather prophets, the countryman and the sailor. These might say with scorn, "Before the scientific weather forecasts, we *knew*."

So farewell to you, poor old Dr. Malcolm! Rest assured that I can now appreciate how much we owed to your most constant care of us!

Time passes—I am nearly thirteen when the doctors who attended my father in his last illness come into my memories of the past. I can see Dr. Peddie passing in and out of my father's bedroom. A little man, grey and austere, a model of professional gravity, dry, perhaps shy, in his manner with children. I associated him with a queer frightened feeling, which I was too young to call anxiety. I knew he had been called in to see my father several times during what seemed to me long months, and each time Ann had told me "Papa" had a pain and had gone to bed. I remember her making hot poultices to ease the pain. She was a great hand at poultices! But always, till now, Papa had recovered, and my frightened feeling had gone with the pain. But this time it was different. This time the pain went on and on, and Dr. Peddie came and came. And always, home from school, my uneasy question, "How's Papa?"

Another doctor comes into that time. One afternoon, when Louis and I were sitting in the old nursery, quiet, in a now alas! too quiet house, Ann opened the door and ushered in an elderly gentleman, clad in the usual black, with a face which I dimly recall as being broad and humorous.

"Doctor John Brown," Ann announced.

I knew the name, but as yet nothing of the fame that went with it. I do not think that in those young days I had read *Rab and his Friends*, but I had heard my father talk of it and had seen the pictures.

It was in the after years that I learned to appreciate that moving little tale of simple folk, and to realise the author's understanding sympathy with the humble sick and sorrowing, and his love of animals. Then, too, I came to know him as one renowned in the medical world, besides being an author of distinction.

Louis and I were glad when he sat down at our table and chatted cheerfully, though all the time it was easy to see that his thoughts were elsewhere, and that he waited for a summons. He took a sheet of paper and a pencil, and sketched for us, in a few clever strokes, the picture of a funny little man, with buttons all down his funny little front, dancing legs and a ridiculous head. Curious, how that sketch is so clear in my mind. Do I associate it, I wonder, with a new awakened sense of anxiety? At the moment it made us laugh, and of course that was what he wanted. As he finished it, Ann came to the door. He rose at once, and throwing over the sketch to us with some gay words, followed her out of the room.

Alas! for my father, alas! for us all, even the knowledge and skill of Dr. John Brown was of no avail, for my father died in the cold of January 1882, on my thirteenth birthday. But because for me, a motherless girl, my father's death was an unforgettable tragedy, so all down the long years I have carried in a grateful heart the names of those two doctors who laboured to save his life.

One other I must speak of who had his part in this sad time. During the months of that unhappy autumn, Louis and I were uneasily conscious of a background of strain in the household, though ignorant of its inevitable end. With an eldest brother at Oxford, and a second busy with his own schoolwork, we should have sorely missed my father's gay companionship in the long evenings and his help in our home-lessons. Into this breach stepped a young man, dear friend of the early years and of many years to come. He was at that time a medical student, able and enthusiastic, probably ambitious, for the day came when Edinburgh knew and honoured him as a professor in her University. For us, he was just "George", who in our crisis laid aside his own plans and purposes, coming evening after evening to sit with us two children while we did our lessons, helping us, playing with us, and so sending us off to bed with the sense of strain lifted from our young hearts. Youth is inarticulate and takes much for granted, but now at long last, I put words to thoughts, saying to George Lovell Gulland "Thanks! and again thanks!" sure that he will know and understand.

Childhood's days fly past, but I am still a schoolgirl when a new and forceful figure comes into my medical memories, comes, and stays, and will stay while I live. Dr. Alexander Bruce, at that time in the earlier stages of a distinguished career, was an Aberdonian, therefore serious. But alongside the seriousness was a keen sense of humour, which would flash out all of a sudden, changing the whole atmosphere of a sickroom. He was a thinker and a teacher, having besides an emotional love of beauty and music. I remember seeing him in tears at the theatre. But above all he was a physician, and it was as a physician that I blessed and do still bless him. But young men who cared for things artistic and intellectual found in him a friend. My brother Harry was one of these.

The first time I met him was when Ann, still our faithful guardian, ever anxious about us, took me on Harry's advice to see him in his house in Alva Street. As we were shown into his consulting-room, there rose from his desk a man of middle height, unusually broad in the shoulder. His hair was brown, red-tinged, above an intellectual forehead. Handsome? I don't think so. Nothing so ordinary. But none could look at that face of his, with the close-shut mouth and heavy-lidded brown eyes, without being made aware that here was a mind and soul of peculiar fineness, set off by an appealing charm of manner. This appreciation of mine must have developed later, as I grew older and knew him better. But even then, though young and immature, I was ardent and responsive to impressions. At this first meeting I was sure that here was one who would be a very present help in trouble. Shy schoolgirl that I was, his grave kindliness put me at ease, and his sudden smile might of itself have wrought cures. I was at the age for hero-worship. Dr. Bruce became my hero. And what confirmed this for me was the way he dealt with Harry, that temperamental, high-strung brother of mine, a scholar, a poet, a creature of strains and stresses, taking him under his wing, becoming for him as a strong tower in the wilderness of worries that afflicted his early manhood, setting him on his feet and on his scholastic way. Harry was dear to me, my adviser among books, my critical guide and mentor in literary taste. His distresses were reflected in me as in a mirror, and his healing lifted my heart and filled it with undying gratitude to the "beloved physician".

As time went on, and I married, and other doctors came into my life, still Dr. Bruce was there. He was there when William went down with scarlet fever, and at once took us both under his cheerful charge, and sent us a nurse with a sense of humour. He had by then attained to high rank as a consultant physician and an extra-mural lecturer. I never understood why he did not become one of our professors. But he had a full life of work and thought, and lively interests. One met him at concerts and operas. He never missed the soul in music, and his was the spirit behind science that makes it a live thing. And though I never heard him speak of it, I divined that he had a deep sense of religion. Possibly stern, but for himself, not for others.

Alas! that the call came when there was still so much for him to do, so much to love, so much to learn, and perhaps with some hopes unfulfilled. But all he did and taught will have borne fruit. It has been left for his successors to realise the hopes. I mourned for one who was untiring, spendthrift, in the cause of high ideals.

It was to Dr. Bruce I owed the only, short and emotional, meeting with Dr. Jessie McGregor, at one time his assistant. My little son was ill, with temperature rising dangerously. Dr. Bruce, unable to come himself, sent his assistant. It was late at night. The atmosphere of the room was heavy with my fears. My husband and I watched and waited. Jessie McGregor came in. As she bent over the crib I noted the absorption of the true physician, and the quiet voice questioning. Here it is enough to say that danger and anxiety fled before her. I thanked her, and him who sent her. I never saw her again. I had been till then distrustful of women doctors, but Jessie McGregor altered my creed. Dr. Bruce believed in her and in her future. She was the friend of Dr. Elsie Inglis, so well known and so blessed by many. But for Jessie McGregor God had other plans. Death claimed her when she was still young and eager. Those who knew her would not forget her.

When I married William, doctor and university lecturer, it was as if I had been made an honorary member of an honourable brotherhood. We lived in George Square, with the Profession hemming us in on every side. Dr. Stewart was a next-door neighbour, and Dr. Matheson's fat old coachman with the silver buttons, waiting in the sunshine before his master's door, gave a touch of old-world splendour to the morning pageant of carriages.

At the opposite side of the Square lived Alexander Miles, the surgeon, and that friendship began which was to last

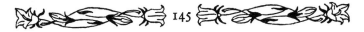

for so many years. Mr. Miles, able, keen and kind, was besides a lover of the Perthshire Highlands, and happy memories come thronging of holidays in the lovely places where the Ardle flows, where his family and ours went a-fishing in the tumbling burns, and we picnicked merrily among the hills. How long ago it seems! Yet how fresh and glowing!

As I sit writing this it seems only the other day when William died in our home in the South, and but a few months later, in Edinburgh, Alexander Miles followed him. Both were full of years, both had been good and faithful in a high service, and surely their works shall follow them.

One must teach oneself to look upon the passing of such as these as the joining up of a goodly company of great souls; so many of them! whom to know was to revere. Should we say *"requiescat in pace"* For men like them? So keen, so courageous, even radiant? Nay, rather let us shout aloud to Heaven "Carry on, brave hearts!"

Two such others come into my mind to whom I personally owe much. Sir Halliday Croom was an extra-mural lecturer and a practitioner in midwifery and gynaecology. I have heard William recall with amused appreciation his stimulating teachings on the adventures of childbirth, laced, so to speak, with arresting anecdotes which gripped and stayed in the memories of his student audience, who were to carry on and develop the wonders of Simpson and Syme and Lister. Sir Halliday had a fine presence, made conspicuous by his habit of wearing an evening-dress coat when lecturing. I can only speak of his personality beside a patient, which seemed like shelter in a storm, inspiring courage, giving one assurance that out of the depths of wisdom would come safety and rejoicing. I can see him now, a robust shirt-sleeved figure, as I struggled out of chloroform unconsciousness, and through the roaring in my ears heard his resonant voice: "You've got a son!"

"Oh, where?" and as I tried to raise myself came the stern command, "Lie still!" and once more the peace of chloroform.

And when it was all over and done with, and I lay exhausted and happy, he took my face between his hands, saying, "You're just a wee baby yourself," and patted my cheek and went.

Then there was the coming of Dr. Milne-Murray on two of the same errands of mercy. One of these was on Christmas Day, 1900, when my son David was born. A joyous day to choose! but one awkward in keeping a doctor away from his own home circle. But Dr. Milne-Murray had no children, which I was told he felt deeply. As he sat by my bedside watching and waiting, my two little ones were brought in for a moment to show themselves in all their glory dressed for a Christmas party. I saw the look in my doctor's eyes, and even with my own insistent preoccupations I felt pity for him. When my Christmas baby was safely there, and he was going, I managed to murmur some apology for spoiling his day. But he only laughed as he bade me good-bye, and wishing me what was left of a "Merry Christmas", added, "and I'll still be in time for Christmas dinner!"

Dr. Milne-Murray made special appeal to a mother's heart, because of the intense interest he took in the baby's welfare. He was learned in feeding lore and discipline. I remember the keen incisiveness with which he used to tell

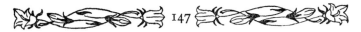

me of his studies in Paris about infant-feeding, and he enthusiastically preached and practised what he had learnt there. I trusted him and greatly admired him. He had a grave Scottish mind, probably inherited from his country school-master father, and how fine a mind *that* can be one has only to read about the "Dominie" in *Beside the bonnie Briar Bush* to find out. He had a burning desire to add to the knowledge of his so-human speciality, and to banish all prejudice in its practice. Women nowadays will hardly believe that even in the latter years of the nineteenth century there were still people who maintained that the unrelieved pains of child-birth were God's will for women. Dr. Milne-Murray fought gallantly on our behalf, scattering folly to the winds, saying boldly that if he had his will he would banish every pain after the first.

His death, all too early, as he was reaching full maturity and authority in a career most blest for women, was a calamity.

As life in all its fullness opened out for me, I found it one of my most interesting and inspiring of duties to visit certain wards in the Royal Infirmary, where so many of the doctors I knew pursued their beneficent way, leaving in their track comfort and grateful hearts. I loved the long rooms with their windows looking out on the green stretches of the Meadows, where on balconies bathed in sunshine happy convalescents lay at ease. I loved the flowers on the tables, the quiet nurses, and the faces that smiled at me from their pillows. Few of those lying there but knew they were the guests of a wide charity, but few would understand that they made their own immeasurable return to humanity, for to their bedsides came the teachers and the taught.

For a number of years I served on the Board of Directors of the Simpson Memorial Maternity Hospital, hearing and taking part in many a grave discussion about the welfare of the women and infants under our charge. Invaluable in our many responsible duties were the help and guidance of the doctors who wrought and taught in the Hospital. Their names are linked in my memory with devoted service. Dr. Haig Ferguson, Dr. Ballantyne, Dr. Haultain and others. Men who daily faced the problems to do with "all women labouring of child", whose minds and hearts were set on making easier the way. How triumphantly one can best judge in the light of modern marvels due to their beginnings. It is true that our doctors differed at times about *how* to achieve the best, never that the best must be achieved. Dr. Watson, eager, able, impatient, came for a season back to his native land from Canada, did great work, and before he returned there, had swept away some cobwebs. Maybe some of us were old-fashioned and rather clung to our cobwebs. But we learned better, looked at what he had done with understanding eyes and saw that it was good.

And there was Dr. Haultain, so strong in his opinion that mothers should be set on their feet almost as soon as the baby was in their arms! Well—from what I learn now, much of the doctrine he preached is the gospel for today.

A few more names, some few more words of thanks, and I shall lay down my pen with a conscience at ease.

Dr. John Thomson—surely many will remember him and his charming wife, she a Highlander from the Hebrides, he so much the Scot, with his accent and his reddish beard, and his stern Free Church outlook but also so much the kind physician and friend of little children. The Children's

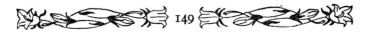

Hospital was his, most fortunate, domain. From there he drew that experience and intimate wisdom so necessary in dealing with a child, and many a little one, mine among them, outside the place of his jurisdiction, benefited. Many a little sick head lately laid low looked up at him with smiles. One of his attributes much impressed me, his swift diagnosis of infectious illness, where he was a magician, so that no early mistake should mar recovery. He and his soft-eyed "Isabel" were our good friends for many a long year.

I don't think Dr. George Carmichael ever forgot that William had been his teacher and guide in the province of pharmacology. The ideals that William believed in he passed on to his pupils, and Dr. Carmichael had grasped and used them to much purpose in his strenuous life as a general practitioner, in which he so ungrudgingly came to my aid in various vicissitudes. He was humble, but sure, and very gentle. A person to like and trust.

And can I ever forget how Mr. Caird, the brilliant surgeon, having about him a sturdy Scottish optimism, so reassuring to an anxious heart, came like a David to challenge the new and dangerous Goliath Appendicitis when my little son lay in his grip, and sent him packing?

One last memory, of the later years, splendid, exciting. The first crisis of grandmotherhood for me loomed close ahead. In a room, high above the Water of Leith, I sat waiting, with beating heart and ears straining for any sound. Silence, after a period of intermittent cries. What was happening? Was all well? And then at last the door opened. I started up, and Professor Johnstone came to me, beaming victory, and holding out hands of congratulation, laughingly announced: "Well, you've got a golliwog for a grandson!"

All good men and true, these doctors of mine, and infinitely kind. Duty wrapped them round, as in a cloak. May Heaven bless them, for I cannot find the words.

And so an end to reminiscence. But there is no ending to a great tradition, for tradition is its own progenitor and parent, giving eager birth to new thought and new experiment, and in that medical world which holds my love and reverence, to an ever closer touch with the things that belong to compassion.

So it has ever been with Edinburgh, the beloved city. So I hope and pray shall it ever be. Surely, surely, one of her inestimable gifts to mankind, can I say the backbone of her fame, has been the sending out into the world doctors of renown, giants in a humane profession. Even to be one of the humblest of her citizens was to bear about one's head some faint reflection, some glimmer, of that aura of distinction. I was conscious of it all the time I lived there. I am even more proudly conscious of it now that I live there no longer.

GOOD AND FAITHFUL SERVANTS

Among women worthy of honour, none seem to me to be
more deserving of high place than the old servants of a
generation ago. The day of such is passing; nay, is already
gone. In these days few indeed will be found who will
sing the praises of that "service of the antique world".
But I, deeming it a beautiful thing, would pay it a
tribute before the memory of it, as I knew it, has quite
faded.

Here will I set down three honourable names, the names
of three young women who, about ninety years ago, and
some fifteen years or so before I was born, came to take
service with my father and mother in a house in Edinburgh
near the Blackford Hill—Ann Torbain, Margaret Forbes,
Christina Morris; plain names, but names almost in themselves an earnest of good behaviour, bearing witness to
decent parentage. Family names known in the countryside
to which they belonged, Christian names given to them
because their forebears had borne them. These had been

L

"Fife folk", and our three were all born in that good King-dom across the Forth, and had in large measure the heritage of her people, wisdom and a shrewd wit. Humble in origin, in their outlook on life and its duties I count them as having been innately noble. Little enough schooling had come their way, but that little had been paid for out of hard-won wages by hard-working parents, who valued education as only Scots can, and passed on their sense of values to their children.

Reverence for learning, and the Fear of God, and our three had both—these surely are the beginning of wisdom. The late Simon Laurie, Professor of Education in Edinburgh University, once said to me that, in his opinion, it was the Shorter Catechism that gave Scottish brains their grit. Perhaps this may account for the sturdy independence of thought and judgment of these three women. They set great store by that independence, and by their self-respect. Loyalty was inherent in their religion, obedience something in their gift. Domestic service meant to them a dedication of peculiar talents, and they had been bred to think that to earn their living in this manner was their high calling. Finding employers kind and generous, they served them generously and honourably with their capable hands and brains, and in response to kindness their warm hearts gave back affection. They were regarded, and regarded them-selves, as members of the family, in whose joys they shared and whose sorrows were to them a personal grief.

Though staunch Presbyterians, and strict in their notions of Sabbath observance, they must also have been unusually wide-minded and tolerant. Not only did they join in our Episcopalian Family Prayers, but they were ever ready with

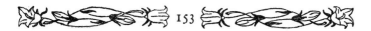

a welcome for our French friends and cousins who came often to stay with us, and who were Roman Catholics and went to early Mass. And Presbyterian Christina never forgot the Catholic Friday fish.

I was sixteen months old when my mother died, bequeathing to Ann the care of the young children and the little new-born son. Into Christina's trustworthy hands my father confided the whole management of the household. A year or two later we moved into the house in York Place which became our home for so long, and where begin my personal memories of the three wonderful women who, for upwards of fifty years, served our family with unsurpassable devotion.

Like one another in the broad ways of faith and conduct, their personalities were distinct and distinctive.

Christina was a little woman, thin and wiry, with dark eyes, usually kindly, but which could sparkle with sudden anger. Of untiring energy, she had an insatiable lust for cleaning and polishing, but she wrought magic by stealth, without fuss or bustle, leaving in her tracks shining floors and gleaming brasses.

We were generally away at Clovenfords during the spring-cleaning season, but I remember coming home to the antiseptic smells, the starched-lace summer curtains, and the rather chilly brilliance which marked the end of that orgy. The sound and fury had passed, and there stood Christina, calm and smiling, once more a conqueror in that grim battle with soot and dust and spiders, looking, in her afternoon cap and apron, just as if nothing unusual had happened.

Christina called herself a "good plain cook", but I know he took immense pride in her pastry and scones, and

achieved miracles in jams, while in the brewing of such
succulent soups as "cocky-leekie" and "hotch-potch" she
was past-mistress.

But she must have risen to more impressive culinary
heights when my father gave a dinner-party. Well do I
remember her on those occasions, when one saw her through
a steamy mist of cookery, moving, stern and silent, amid a
welter of plates and dishes, stirring gravies and mixing
sauces, and all to the merry music of bubblings and sizzlings
and in the almost tropical heat of the open range.

Christina was shy in speech, with a prim English for good
manners, but when roused or occasion served, she could
make racy use of her native Scots. She abhorred what she
called "Sinfu' waste", and the saving of coal was a passion.
To poke the fire into a blaze after she had put on the
"gathering" lump, and doused it well down with a shovelful
of "sma" was in her eyes crime unspeakable. The chilly but
rash sinner was sternly rebuked.

"Laddie! can ye no' leave the fire alane?"

Jealous in the matter of the family reputation and dignity,
she was horrified to see my brother run out in his bedroom
slippers to post a letter—"Shaughlin' aboot in a pair o'
bauchles!" she protested indignantly.

I have a memory of her in later days, when we, grown
daintier than our elders had been, had disapproved of some
dish she had sent up to table—we summoned her to the
dining-room. She came and stood, neat and trim, and a
trifle grim, half in and half out of the door. There was battle
in her eye. We made our complaint, and she listened,
ominously silent, till we had done. Then, while we waited
for apology or excuse at least:

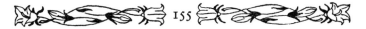

"Ye're jist a set o' fashious deevils!" she flung at us, and vanished, closing the door gently behind her.

She was a famous marketer, and not the most truculent of butchers or bakers could beat her at a bargain. It was my delight as a child to go with her to the Waverley Market early on a summer Saturday morning. I see her now, in her little black bonnet, a shawl over her print "wrapper", and an enormous double-lidded market basket over her left arm. For me, that market, with its smells of green things and ripe strawberries, the early sunlight coming through the glass roof, the carts of produce and the stamping of farm-horses in the lane, was all excitement. For Christina it was a happy hunting-ground. She was like the war-horse, snuffing the battle from afar. Her keen eye would appraise the heaps of potatoes on some country grower's stall, and she would stand over him critically watching the weighing out of pecks of peas, while her shrewd tongue daunted him into taking a halfpenny or two off his price before allowing him to fill up that mammoth basket of hers with the small red strawberries which she called "scaurlets". Then she would give a queer, dry little laugh, her song of triumph.

Christina's age was always a mystery—we could never find out, and I remember my father laughing over a census paper and saying that ten years never made any difference to Christina! She must have been pretty elderly when I married and she went to keep house for my brothers in a flat in Great King Street. When at last she retired on her well-earned pension and lived in Gilmour Place, various nieces cared for her and she had all she wanted. She had ever been thrifty, and her needs were simple. She delighted to welcome me and make me a cup of tea and hear about my children. When she died, a group of her well-to-do relations gathered round her grave and praised her to my brother, speaking of her long service in our family with pride and admiration. But to this day I do not know how old she was.

Fine, loyal, fierce, warm-hearted creature! I have never met her like.

My childish memories of Forbes (we never called her Margaret) centre to a large extent round my father's dinner-parties. In housewifely ways she was an artist, and parties must have been for her artistic adventures, giving full scope to her talents. Set ready by her hands, the early Victorian drawing-room, with its white and gold walls, rose-pink sofa and chairs, glittering steel-grate reflecting a blazing fire, took on so charming an air of warmth and brilliance that it seemed the completely proper setting for the shimmering silks and satins of the ladies. In the dining-room the long table laid for eighteen guests sparkled with the glass and silver, which were her pride and joy—Many's the time did I, a little girl from the nursery, steal downstairs, and with Forbes holding my hand, peep in to see and admire the glittering glory of her achievement!

In appearance, Forbes was handsome, with a fine dignity of demeanour. She was clever, and she was wise, with something of grandeur and passion in her temperament. She was a native of St. Andrews, and I cannot but think that those born in the shadow of that lovely ghost Cathedral, and familiar with the cliffs and links, the sea and the wide skies, which make the setting of that grey city of learning, must inherit something of her spirit. Forbes was deeply aware of the beauty of Scottish song and scenery, and it is to her I owe much of my own love for all things Highland, mountains and heather, the smell of peat and the skirl of the pipes. Our maids shared in all our holidays and picnics, and while on these occasions my memory pictures Christina weighed down with her enormous basket stuffed full of picnic fare, and Ann wandering along, her arms laden with our discarded coats, I seem to see Forbes enthusiastically picking blue-bells in the Aberdour woods, or brambles on the 'bonny bonny banks', or even mushrooms on the island of Kerrera. In her busy active life Forbes must have found time to read, and time to listen; and there must have been much to listen to in our house, for my father entertained many guests with many and varied interests, and as she waited on them at dinner Forbes would hear much talk and many an argument, and find food for her own intelligent mind—for she would talk about Sir Walter Scott and *The Lady of the Lake* when we had a day's outing to the Trossachs, and she and I walked on the "Silver Strand" and gazed across to "Ellen's Isle"—and deeply graven into my consciousness of these early years are some of the lovely things of Burns, and I feel sure that it was Forbes who sang to me of the "red red rose", and taught me to know the daisy as the "crimson-tippèd" flower.

My schoolboy brother Charlie was what would now be called a theatre "fan". So was Forbes, and many's the Saturday evening they two would go off to the pit of the Theatre Royal, and there, refreshed by oranges, they would sit enthralled through many a forgotten play. Are there any still alive who remember "Poor Joe" and "Colleen Bawn"?

Well on in life Forbes married a retired engine-driver, and they went to live in Pittenweem. There, in a little house, at the top end of a little row of houses, they dwelt together for a number of happy years, in a peace seasoned with humour and a pleasant content with simple things. Just beside their little home ran the single railway line to St. Andrews, and there the erstwhile engine-driver could, if so minded, watch the infrequent trains go by, and ponder, as he smoked his pipe in quietness, of the days when he too drove an engine; while Forbes, standing at her own door, could look down the road and away to the grey Forth, where she might see the brown-sailed fishing-boats come slipping into harbour, and hear the sound of waves lapping a sandy shore.

And how at last shall I come to speak of Ann?

Ann, the beloved nurse, the almost mother to us, the motherless? Ann, the comforter and friend, the much-loving and the dearly loved for so many long years? She it was who received into her adoring arms each child of us within an hour of birth: she it was who, when two of my brothers and my only sister lay sick of a fever, tended them with untiring devotion, and when nothing availed to save them wept at the side of the stricken parents. And when my mother was dying it was on Ann's breast she lay, and heard her promise never to leave us so long as we had need of her. With ever grateful heart I can bear witness to the faithful courage with which she fulfilled that promise.

She was of different fibre from Christina and Forbes, a creature of love and emotion, with a soul full of pity, finding it difficult to be stern. Behind her was a story of tragedy. Too greatly loving, she had in her early years given herself to the young man who was to have married her, and he was killed in an accident at his work before they were wed. In her mother's home she bore his son, and must needs earn money for him. My mother was told this story, and in deep

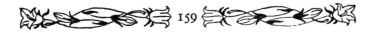

compassion sent for her, and kept her, earning thereby the selfless gratitude and devotion of a gentle being, and winning for us, when she herself had gone, that most rare blessing for her children, a settled background of nursery security and routine.

Far back, and deep down in my earliest consciousness, is my awareness of Ann. Ann always there, a pervading presence. Ann, a refuge in the dark, the consoler in hurts and troubles. Ann, dressing us, washing us, scolding us, drying our tears, teaching us pretty ways, mindful of our manners, guardian standing between us and the rough world outside. Pictures of Ann in these early years come crowding to my mind. Vivid pictures, remaining for me unforgettable memories. I see her, busy in the morning with broom and duster, with us children playing round her feet. Again, in the afternoon, neat and sweet with her black silk apron on, knitting by the fire, or with me on her lap, reading to me. She was no scholar, but she had imagination, and the feeling heart came through the careful sentences, keeping me happy and enthralled. In such wise did I hear and absorb many an old nursery classic. Watt's Hymns, Mrs. Barbauld's Hymns in Prose, Miss Edgeworth's "Rosamund" stories.

Ann was a very simple person, humble in her own esteem, with a wisdom intuitive rather than deliberate. She had a leaning towards melancholy, like many Scots—but she had a fine, brave cheerfulness too, especially in emergencies, a quality of the soul, not the outcome of mere lightheartedness. Her laughter, never loud, would often end in a sigh, as if she looked back over her shoulder at some spectre of sadness. And I sometimes wonder if when she looked at us children she saw our innocent heads against a background of bereavement, making her cherish us the more. Was this perhaps in her mind when she took us for walks in the Grange Cemetery? Most Scots find a solemn joy in contemplation among the tombs. But I think the call for Ann was more direct. She would lead us along the quiet paths to that plot of ground which we knew as "ours", and which my memory sees bathed in perpetual sunshine and peace, and there she would stand and gaze at the low white headstone which bore my mother's name, and at the white marble cross with the names of those children, my only sister and two of my brothers whom she had loved and nursed before we were born. What visions of anxious days and nights, of parents' agony and tears must these names have conjured up for Ann! Did she think that in this way she might help create in us, the youngest-born, who had no actual memory of those earlier days, a sort of spiritual memory, linking us to those who belonged to us and to whom we belonged?

For Ann the ever-present realisation that in the midst of life we are in death I am sure gave an added spice to life. Drama played its part. And this fits in with certain vivid memories of tearful ladies, family friends, who came sometimes to visit us in the nursery and drink a cup of Ann's tea, where, sitting in their silks and furs, they would speak in mournful undertones of illness and death, shedding luxurious tears between sips of tea, and finding in Ann a deeply sympathetic listener.

When I was thirteen my father died. Through a long illness Ann nursed him, tending him night and day. To the end he would have no other nurse.

In my bewilderment and a child's agony of loss I clung to Ann. In such a crisis she showed extraordinary power to

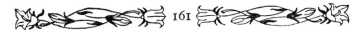

uphold and strengthen—and yet I smile now when I remember the fond pride with which she dressed me in my new black frock, bedewing it and me with tears.

As the years passed, it was I who became Ann's chief care and charge. All through my girlhood's days, just as in the days of childhood, Ann is always there. Many people, many new influences, came into my life, but she had no possessive jealousy. She loved me, let others love me. She had an open mind and a wide sympathy, and that friends should be generous to me in kindness and counsel seemed to her only right and proper. Her interest was keen in all that interested me. She listened when I aired my immature opinions, and I heard from her many a shrewd comment while she brushed my hair or laced up the satin bodices of my dancing-frocks. The news of my engagement to be married gave her great joy. I still have the letter she wrote to me then. She had not the pen of a ready writer, but here her love and happiness overflowed, covering four pages, triumphing over mistakes in spelling and punctuation, even gaining from them, as if scorning all checks to the rush of feeling that must find an outlet.

She followed me to my married home in George Square, and I rejoice when I think of the happy years she lived with me, taking over the burden of a new nursery which she only laid down when she had reached the age of seventy. But even then, in her happy retirement beside a devoted sister, the new generation filled her heart and her thoughts. They would sit on her knee, just as I had done, and listen to the old stories and nursery rhymes. She knitted their stockings and boasted of their curls.

Ann, dear Ann, though unlearned as the world counts

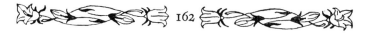

learning, yet walked in such a light of love and unselfishness, in such a knowledge of the human heart, with such intense and wide sympathies that, as I look back, I remember her as one of the wisest and best women I ever knew.

So, "Hail! and farewell" to you, Ann, Christina and Forbes, you three wonderful women. Surely and in truth you were good and faithful servants. What better praise then can I proffer than the words of that long-ago Master? Therefore, with a full heart, I say to you, "Well done".